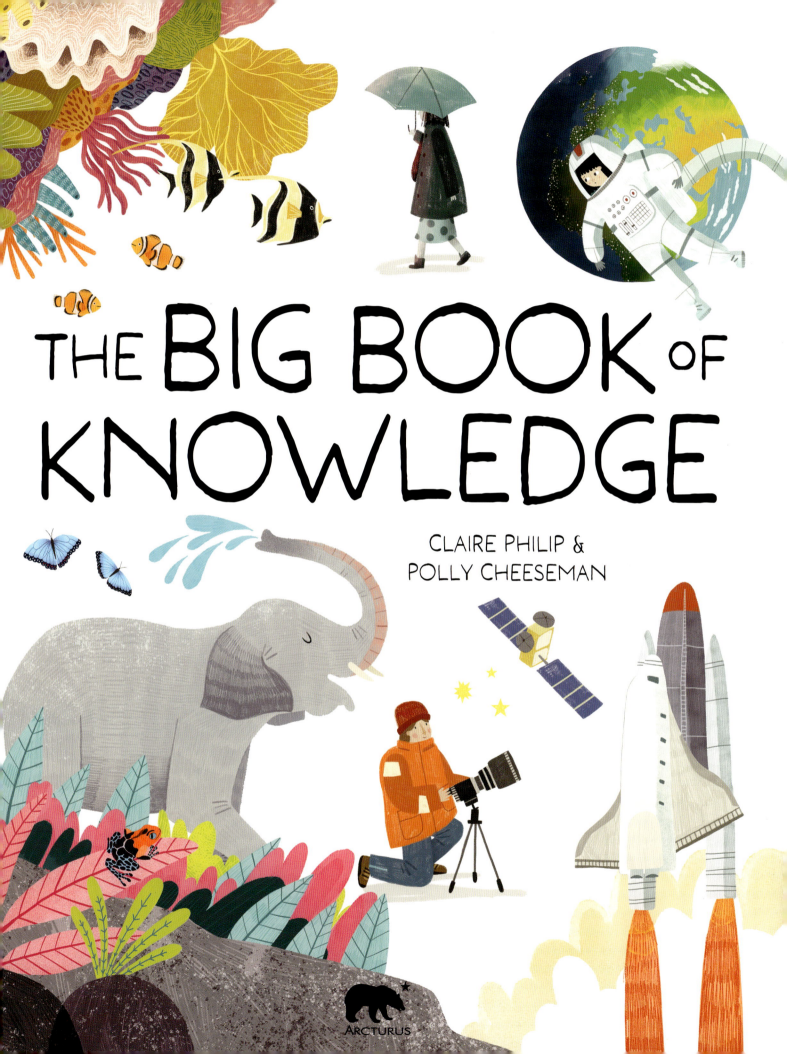

THE BIG BOOK OF KNOWLEDGE

CLAIRE PHILIP &
POLLY CHEESEMAN

ARCTURUS

Arcturus

This edition published in 2024 by Arcturus Publishing Limited
26/27 Bickels Yard, 151–153 Bermondsey Street,
London SE1 3HA

Authors: Claire Philip and Polly Cheeseman
Illustrator: Jean Claude
Editors: Violet Peto and Becca Clunes
Designers: Trudi Webb, Stefan Holliland, Sally Bond, and Paula Crossley
Editorial Manager: Joe Harris

ISBN: 978-1-3988-4665-4
CH011501NT
Supplier 29, Date 0624, PI 00007492

Printed in China

CONTENTS

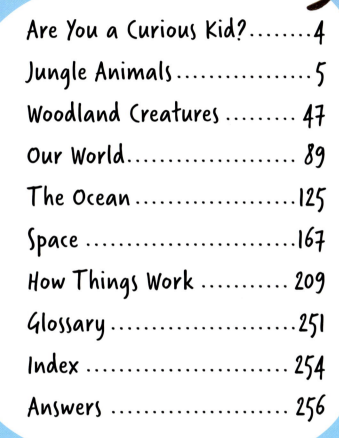

ARE YOU A CURIOUS KID?

Do you love to ask questions and find out about the world?
This book is filled with all kinds of information on different topics.
Here are some of the questions that you can find the answers to.

Where is Earth in the Solar System?

How do astronauts eat in space?

Why do beavers build dams?

How do clocks tell the time?

Which sea creature has a head the shape of a hammer?

Why do chameleons have long tongues?

JUNGLE ANIMALS

JUNGLE HOMES

Many animals make their homes in the jungle.

Birds build neat nests from sticks and leaves.

Jaguars don't need nests. They sleep on the branches of trees.

Termites are tiny insects. They build tall towers from soil, with big rooms underneath.

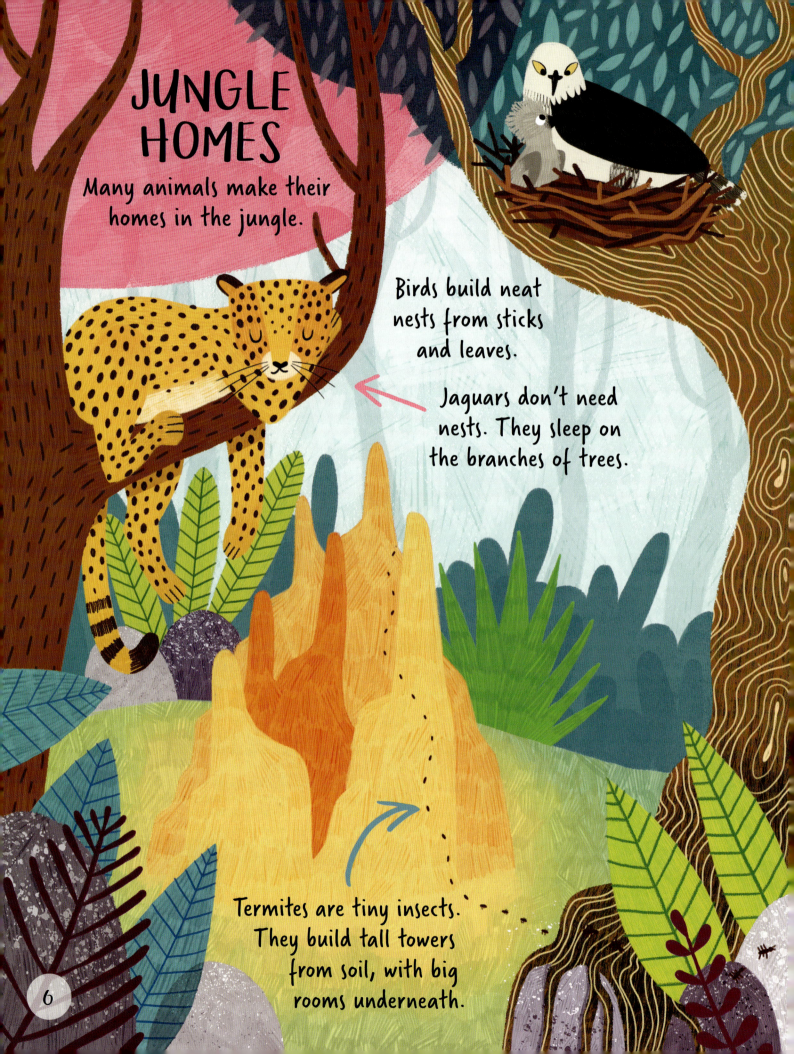

6

The treetops are a perfect home for monkeys. They find lots to eat there.

Some birds, such as parrots, nest in holes in tree trunks.

Tapirs live on the forest floor. They sometimes hide among bushes.

Tiny tree frogs live on leaves. The leaves keep them nice and damp.

ON THE FOREST FLOOR

On the dark, damp rain forest floor, very few green plants grow.

Peccaries, a type of wild pig, use their snouts to snuffle along as they search for food.

Cute agoutis spend time here, too, searching for fallen brazil nuts to chew open with their strong teeth.

Rotting leaves and fungi cover the ground, making a home for all kinds of insects, such as the many-legged giant centipede.

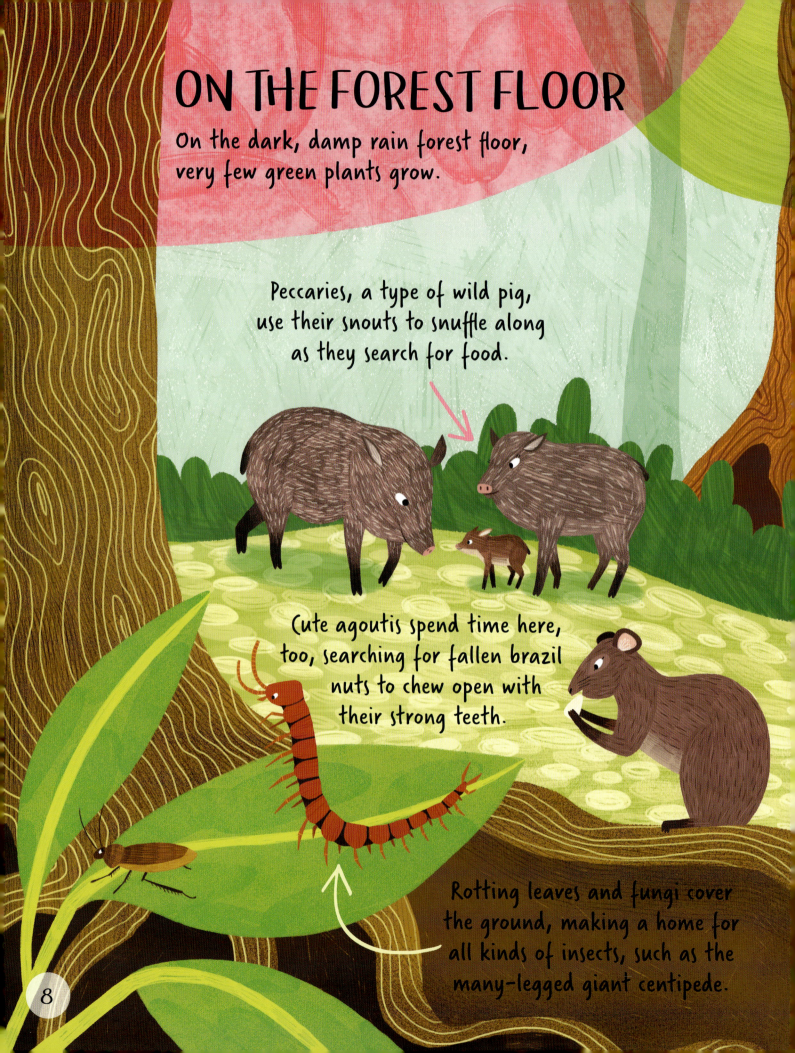

Larger animals, such as ocelots, linger in this part of the jungle. They have excellent eyesight to help them see in the low light.

Bushmaster snakes lay their eggs on the forest floor. The females coil up on top of the nest to protect the babies growing inside.

Goliath bird-eating spiders scuttle along the earth and rest under large leaves.

Leaf-litter toads blend into their homes, making them hard for anyone to spot.

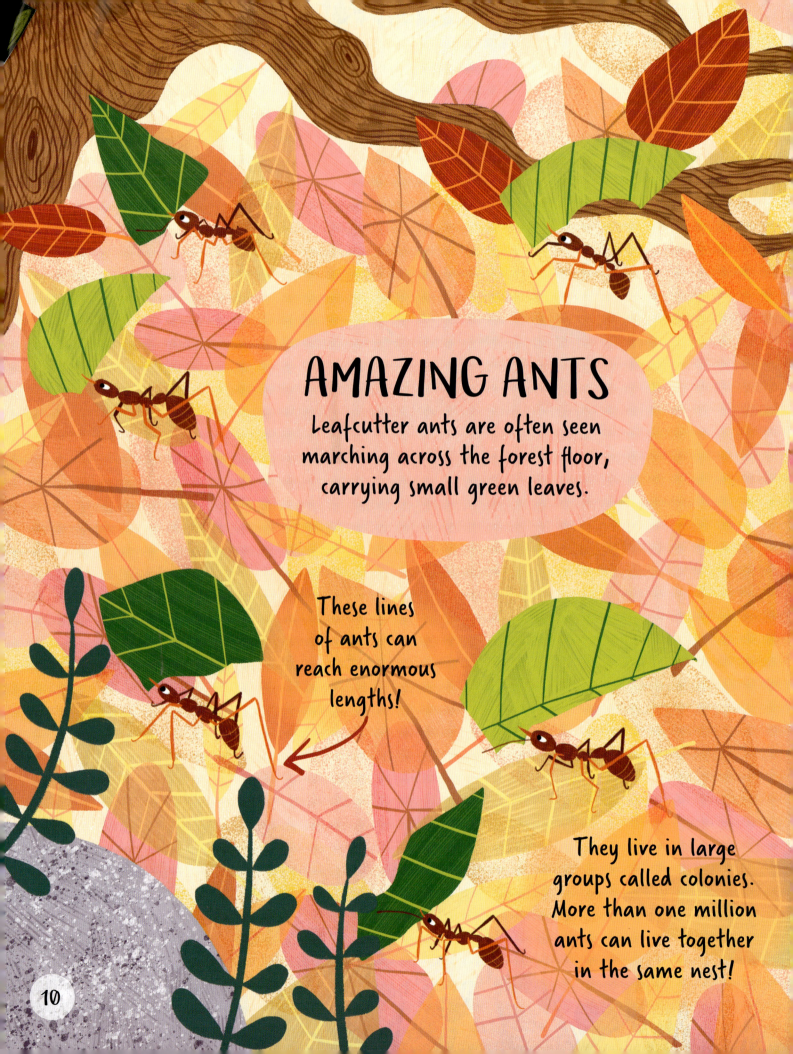

AMAZING ANTS

Leafcutter ants are often seen marching across the forest floor, carrying small green leaves.

These lines of ants can reach enormous lengths!

They live in large groups called colonies. More than one million ants can live together in the same nest!

The ants carry the leaves back to the nest and place them in a special area that is sometimes called a fungus garden.

In the nest, the leaves grow a fungus, which feeds the colony.

Leafcutter ants themselves are food for many jungle creatures, including giant anteaters.

The anteater uses its long tongue to slurp the ants into its mouth.

TERRIFIC TIGERS

Bengal tigers hide in the grasses of Asian rain forests.

Amazingly, no two tigers have the same pattern of stripes.

Their patterns make them hard to spot, so they can easily sneak up on prey.

An adult tiger's roar is very loud. It can be heard a few miles away!

Cubs have even more stripes than adults to give them better camouflage.

Tigers will travel many miles for a meal, and attack under the cover of night.

Tigers hunt many animals, such as monkeys, birds, and even elephants!

Young tiger cubs play-fight together to prepare for attacking prey.

When they are ready, the cubs leave their mothers to find their own areas to hunt in.

13

GREAT GORILLAS

Gorillas are some of the most powerful, yet gentle animals of the rain forest. They are closely related to you and me!

Gorillas are a type of animal called an ape.

In the morning, jungle gorillas sit and eat.

They mostly eat plants, fruit, tree bark, and insects.

Gorillas build large "nests" from plants and trees on the forest floor.

In the afternoon, they sleep, play, and groom each other.

At night, they sleep in their snug nests.

Gorillas live in family groups, usually with one male leader called a silverback.

ON THE RIVERBANK

On a rain forest riverbank, many animals come together to sunbathe, drink, hunt, or play.

Dwarf caiman are members of the alligator family. They build burrows underwater and rest there until they are ready to eat.

River otters play-fight in the water. They are much safer from their big cat predators in the river.

Female giant Amazon River turtles swim along looking for a sunny riverbank where they can lay their eggs.

The river is a great place for predators to hunt, because they can sneak up on prey as they drink from the water.

Capybaras are animals that look like large guinea pigs. They spend most of their time grazing in the thick plants nearby.

Huge green anacondas move more quickly in the water than on land, so they like to swim here.

Red-bellied piranha fish swarm together, using their sharp teeth to snap at other fish and insects.

Manatees poke their funny noses out of the water to breathe.

Small groups spend their days and nights together, nibbling on underwater plants.

When food is hard to find, they live off their large stores of body fat.

MAGICAL MANATEES

Amazonian manatees, or sea cows, swim in freshwater lagoons in the rain forest.

These calm animals are very shy and secretive, and they move very slowly, which makes them easy to hunt.

According to legend, pink river dolphins look after and protect the Amazonian manatee.

These large, beautiful dolphins are very rare today—if you spot one, you are lucky.

19

DEADLY JAGUARS

Jaguars are the third-biggest cats in the world, after lions and tigers.

Jaguars prefer to live alone. They mark their own areas in the forest by leaving claw marks up trees.

Jaguars can hunt very large prey, such as this caiman.

This caiman can grow as long as a giraffe is tall, and has thick, protective skin.

Jaguars have beautiful patterns on their fur—black spots shaped like roses.

Jaguars are very good swimmers. They will sometimes swim through rivers to get close to their prey.

Caimans come out at night to hunt in the water, which is when the jaguar lies in wait.

The jaguar must deliver a deadly bite to the caiman to win its dinner. There is often a long fight.

21

IN THE UNDERSTORY

The understory is an area above the forest floor, where the bushes and grasses grow.

Strange-looking Amazon salamanders climb in this layer.

Greater bulldog bats fly through the understory on their way to lagoons, where they hunt for fish.

Here, many animals live in the trees and bushes.

22

This praying mantis can blend in with the leaves perfectly to hide from prey.

Red-eyed tree frogs sit on plants. They catch bugs with their long, sticky tongues.

Hercules beetles crawl along the branches. They are among the biggest types of flying beetles in the world.

23

POISONOUS FROGS

Poison dart frogs are tiny. They are about the same size as an adult's thumbnail!

They can be yellow, red, green, blue— even gold and black.

Their bright patterns warn other animals that they are dangerous to eat.

Like other frogs, poison dart frogs lay eggs that hatch into tadpoles.

The golden poison dart frog is the most poisonous of all—if a person touches it, they will become very sick.

The tadpoles live in small pools of rainwater that collect inside trees and plants.

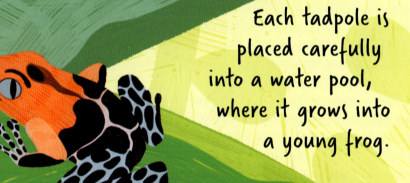

Each tadpole is placed carefully into a water pool, where it grows into a young frog.

Eggs are laid on a damp leaf. Once they hatch, the parents take the tadpoles to pools of water by carrying them on their backs .

SCALY CHAMELEONS

In the forests of Madagascar, off the coast of Africa, lives the panther chameleon.

A chameleon's skin can change from brown to green or orange depending on its mood.

They live up in the trees and have special feet that allow them to grip tightly onto the branches.

Chameleons have skin made of lots of little bumps called scales.

Their tongues can be longer than their bodies!

Moths flutter all over the jungle—they are great snacks for chameleons.

The chameleon shoots out its long, sticky tongue to grab its prey.

A chameleon's amazing eyes can move separately, giving them excellent eyesight.

Emerald tree boas curl up on thick jungle branches. They usually live alone in the wild.

Their long, bright-green bodies have a white zigzag pattern.

Young boas have red bodies with white zigzags. They become green as they grow into adults.

SLITHERING SNAKES

Rain forest snakes often have green bodies to help them blend in with the leaves. This makes it hard for birds of prey to spot and catch them.

First, a boa bites its prey. Then it squeezes the prey until it stops moving.

Boas can sense the body heat from nearby prey, such as mice. Then they strike with their sharp teeth, or fangs.

Once the prey has been swallowed, the snake is full for weeks or even months.

Lots of fruit grows in the canopy, so it's a great place for animals to find food.

Toco toucans use their long beaks to pick and peel fruit.

Spider monkeys play together in the branches, hanging from their strong tails.

Weaver ants make nests here using special silk to glue leaves together.

Saki monkeys hardly ever come down to the ground.

IN THE CANOPY

High up in the trees, above the understory is the leafy canopy. It's the busiest place in the jungle!

Eyelash viper snakes lie in wait for prey. Then— snap! They bite it with their fangs.

Little hummingbirds drink sweet nectar from flowers.

31

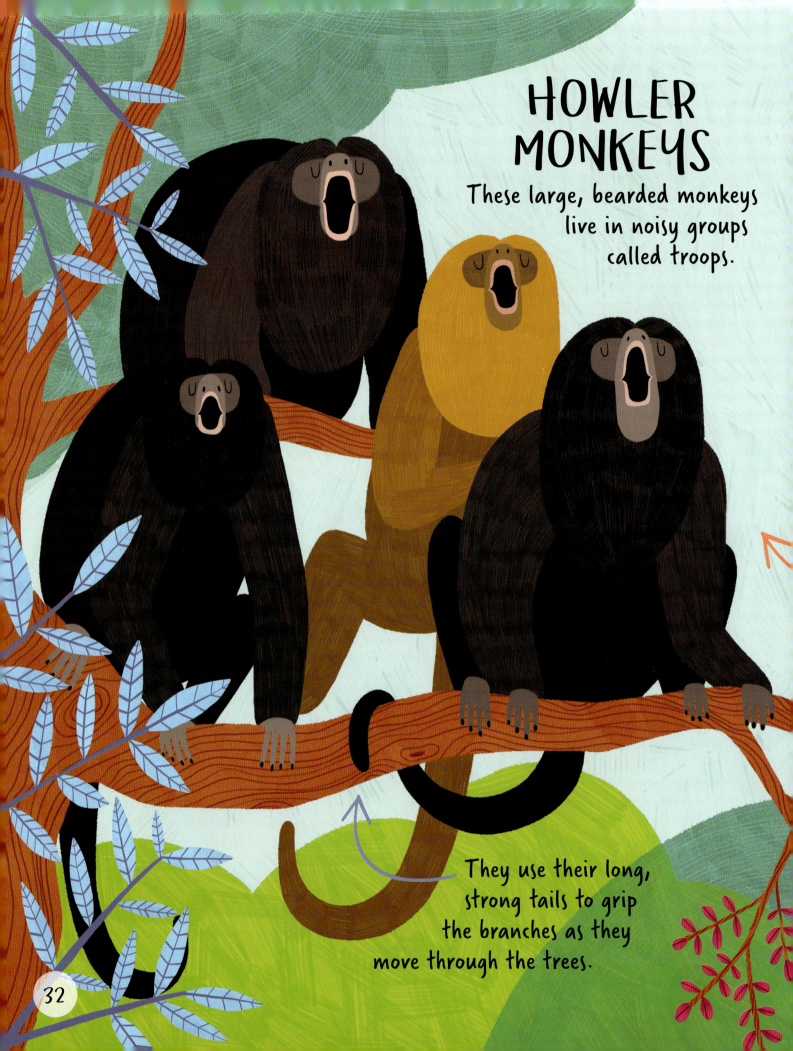

HOWLER MONKEYS

These large, bearded monkeys live in noisy groups called troops.

They use their long, strong tails to grip the branches as they move through the trees.

32

Howler monkeys can have black, red, or brown fur.

They warn other monkeys to stay away by making very loud calls, or howls, which can be heard for miles around.

The males have extra-large throats to help make the noise.

Howler monkeys have an excellent sense of smell, which they use to track down food. They love to eat fruits, flowers, and nuts.

BIRDS OF PARADISE

Birds of paradise are some of the most amazing rain forest birds of all.

Years ago, people thought that these birds came from the heavens, or "paradise."

The female has dull, brown feathers, since she doesn't need to impress a male.

She also looks after the chicks.

Male birds of paradise have bright and fancy feathers which they show off to attract a female.

This male raggiana bird of paradise claps his wings and shakes his head to impress a female.

35

SLOW-MOVING SLOTHS

Sloths are sleepy, tree-dwelling creatures that rarely come down to the ground.

They only visit the forest floor once a week—to go to the toilet!

Green algae grows on their fur. This gives them a green tinge, which helps them blend in with the trees.

Amazingly, lots of other creatures can live on sloths' bodies, such as moths and other insects.

To save energy, sloths move very, very slowly through the forest, but when they swim, they are fairly speedy.

Sloths have very long claws, which they use to grip onto branches as they rest.

Eagles and big cats hunt the sloth.

Sloths mostly eat plants— especially the buds and leaves.

AWESOME ORANGUTANS

Orangutans are known for their orange hair.
They live high up in the tallest trees, yet they do
sometimes visit the forest floor.

They swing from branch to branch
as they search for delicious
fruits to eat.

The babies
hold on tightly
to their mothers
until they are a
few years old.

38

An orangutan's strong arms stretch out longer than the length of its body!

At night, they sleep in snug nests, which they make from branches and leaves.

Orangutans mostly live alone, unless they are taking care of their young.

Their only predators are leopards and other big cats.

Some orangutans have lost their homes because the forests they live in are being cut down.

39

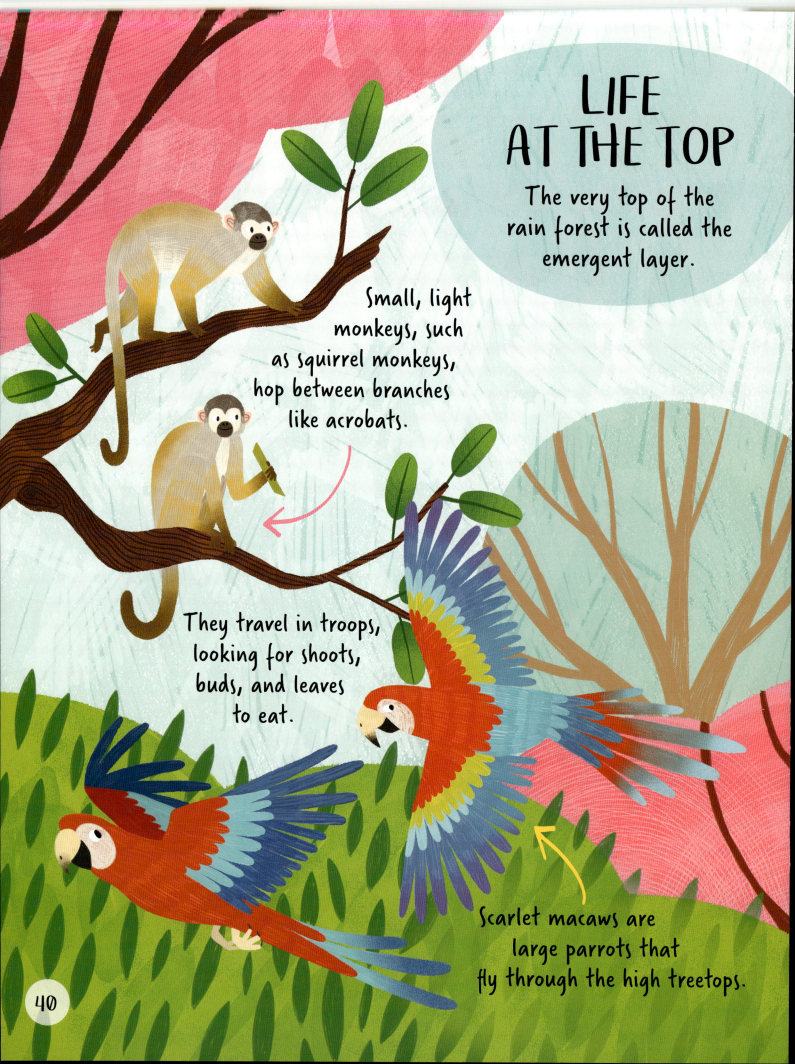

LIFE AT THE TOP

The very top of the rain forest is called the emergent layer.

Small, light monkeys, such as squirrel monkeys, hop between branches like acrobats.

They travel in troops, looking for shoots, buds, and leaves to eat.

Scarlet macaws are large parrots that fly through the high treetops.

The tallest jungle plants of all are found here, such as Brazil nut trees and kapok trees.

The animals that make it this high get the most sunlight—and rain.

Vampire bats often hunt on the ground, but they can be found this high up, too.

Monkeys, such as clever capuchins, collect nuts and fruit.

BRILLIANT BUTTERFLIES

The blue morpho butterfly is one of the largest and most beautiful insects in the rain forest.

Pilots flying planes over the jungle often spot large groups of these butterflies from above.

The tops of their wings are bright blue. Underneath, they are brown, with spots that look like eyes, to put off predators.

From wing to wing, they are the length of a banana!

The butterflies taste their food with their feet! They smell the air with their antennae.

Groups of these butterflies flutter throughout the layers of the forest, from top to bottom.

43

FIERCE EAGLES

Few other jungle birds fly as high as the fierce harpy eagle.

A super-hunter, it perches on top of the tallest rain forest trees to look out for animals to eat.

Harpy eagles will catch and eat smaller birds, iguanas, monkeys— and even sloths!

Not many animals hunt the eagle. It would be too difficult to catch!

Harpy eagles hunt while they fly and use their enormous claws, or talons, to grip onto prey.

A male and female pair will usually stay together for life, raising a chick every few years.

The chick stays in the nest for about a year. Its parents bring meat to feed it.

The female is almost twice the size of the male, yet both are very fast fliers.

45

JUNGLE ANIMALS QUIZ

How well do you remember facts about jungle animals?
Decide if these sentences are true or false, then check
your answers on page 256.

1 The male harpy eagle is bigger than the female.

2 Orangutans are black apes.

3 Sloths move very quickly.

4 Male birds of paradise show off their feathers to attract a female.

5 Howler monkeys warn other monkeys to stay away by making loud calls.

6 Toucans love to eat fruit.

7 Chameleons have long, sticky tongues.

8 Jaguars have black spots shaped like stars on their fur.

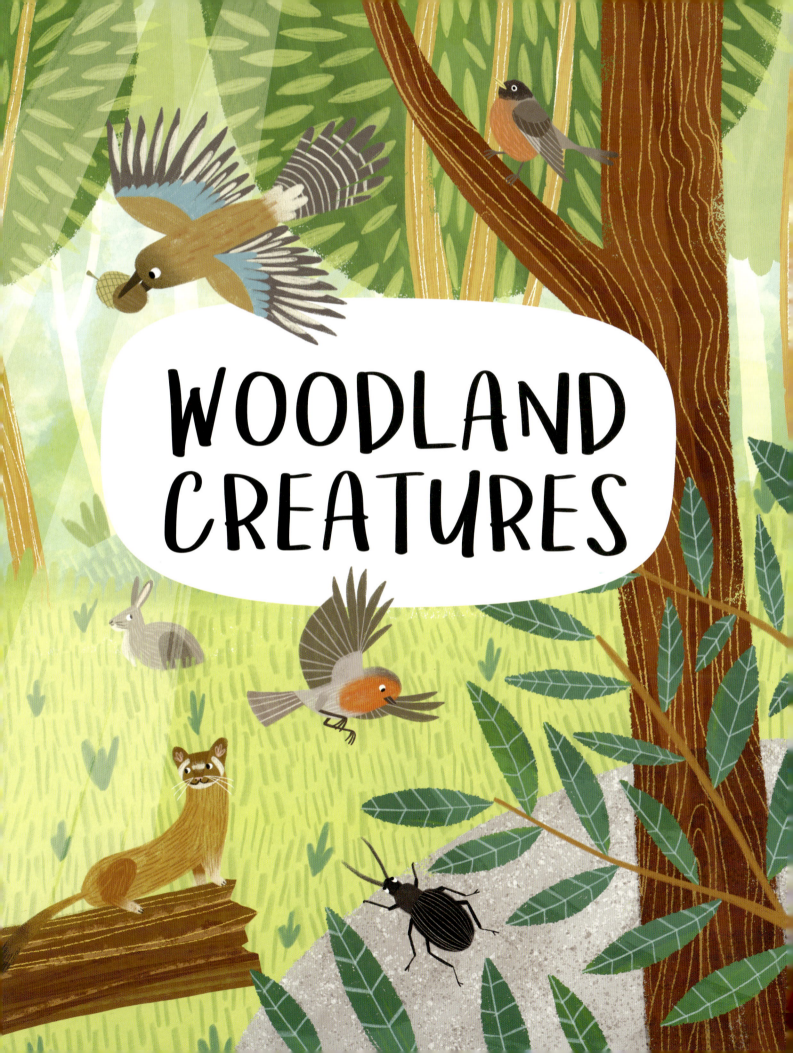

WOODLAND CREATURES

WHAT IS A WOODLAND?

Woodlands and forests are places that are covered in trees. Most woodlands are made up of lots of different species (types) of trees and plants.

In some woodlands, trees stay green all year round. These are called coniferous forests.

Other woodlands, known as deciduous forests, change from season to season.

All kinds of creatures, from woodpeckers and badgers to snakes and butterflies, make woodlands their home.

The trees give the animals shelter and food.

The woodland creatures tidy up the forest. Wriggling worms eat up the rotting plants.

49

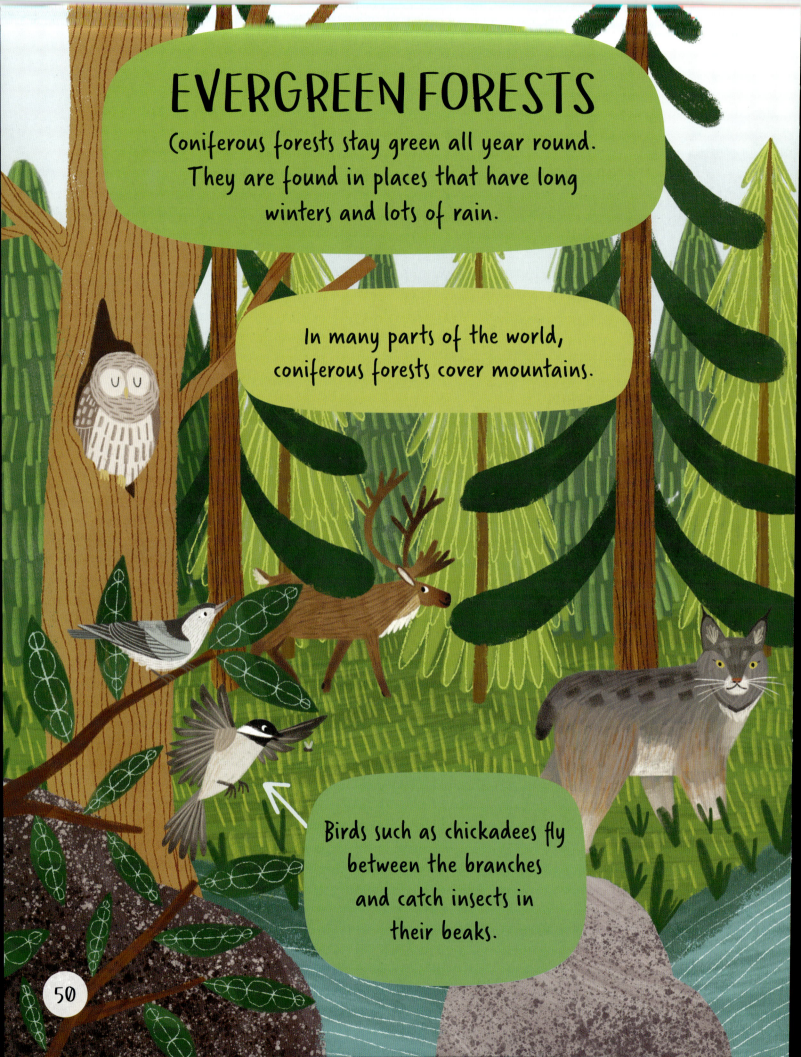

EVERGREEN FORESTS

Coniferous forests stay green all year round. They are found in places that have long winters and lots of rain.

In many parts of the world, coniferous forests cover mountains.

Birds such as chickadees fly between the branches and catch insects in their beaks.

50

Hawks swoop between the tall trees.

Large animals such as lynx, caribou—and even wolves and bears—roam these forests.

The trees that grow in coniferous forests, such as pines, firs, and larches, have leaves all year.

CHANGING SEASONS

In a deciduous forest, the trees lose their leaves when the months get colder. Deciduous forests look very different with each season.

In winter, the trees have no leaves, and there is little life on the ground.

In spring, new leaves grow, and the forest floor is covered with flowers.

In summer, the berries grow on bushes, and trees become heavy with nuts and fruit.

As it starts to get cold, the ground is an orange-brown carpet of fallen leaves.

Deciduous woodlands make perfect homes for deer, weasels, rabbits, robins, wood frogs, and more!

53

ON THE FOREST FLOOR

The forest floor is covered with dead wood and fallen leaves, called leaf litter.

Worms and snails help clean up the forest floor by eating up the rotting plant life.

Fungi grow on fallen trees. They make a special juice that breaks down dead wood.

Lots of different insects and spiders creep across the ground.

Worms, millipedes, and earwigs search for food to eat here.

The forest floor is cool and damp, making it a perfect place for frogs to live.

Snakes such as adders can hide easily among the leaf litter.

THE AMAZING UNDERGROWTH

The shady bottom layer of a woodland is called the undergrowth.

Here, lots of animals look for nuts and berries to eat.

Wild boar snuffle around searching for beechnuts, which fall from beech trees.

Rabbits and hares are also found here, munching on grass.

Badgers roam around at dusk and dawn. They mostly eat earthworms.

Caterpillars crawl over leaves and nettles.

UP HIGH

Animals such as squirrels, bats, and many birds make their homes high up in the trees.

Blackbird chicks learn to fly soon after hatching.

Owls sleep in nooks in the trees during the day. They mostly come out to hunt at night.

Squirrels use moss and twigs to build nests called dreys up in the treetops. When it is cold, squirrels sometimes share dreys for warmth.

A woodpecker nest is simply a hole in a tree, high off the ground. Woodpeckers take turns fetching food for their chicks.

59

FOLLOW THE TRACKS

If you look closely at mud on the forest floor,
you can find footprints left behind by
many different animals.

Deer hooves leave two
long marks, usually with
a point at the front.

Pheasant footprints,
like lots of bird tracks,
look like arrow heads.

60

Fox tracks show four toes in a kind of diamond shape.

Some birds, such as the jay, leave tracks behind in the form of dropped food, such as acorns.

Badgers leave behind large claw marks that look like a cat's, but bigger.

61

NUTS AND BERRIES

Woodlands are great places for animals to find plenty of nuts, seeds, and berries to eat.

Deer wander the forests looking for flowers, berries, bark, and nuts to nibble on.

After eating berries, the seeds pass through an animal's body and out in its droppings.

The seeds in the droppings grow into new plants, and the woodland continues to grow.

Wood mice eat nuts that they store away in their underground burrows.

Waxwings eat a lot of fruit, so their beaks can open unusually wide to help them eat large berries.

HUNGRY HUNTERS

Woodlands are home to many animals that hunt for food.

It can be hard work to chase and catch dinner, so hunters have special features to help them.

Wolves hunt in groups called packs. The packs work together as a team to find food.

Golden eagles have excellent eyesight.

They can spot prey such as rabbits from a long way away, as they soar above the trees.

Sharp claws called talons can easily grab and hold on to prey.

After a long chase, wolves use their strong, sharp teeth to catch their dinner. It can be as big as an elk or a moose!

WOODLAND DIARY: OCTOBER

As the weather gets cooler, the leaves in a deciduous forest turn golden, red, and brown before they fall to the ground.

Insects such as wasps buzz around eating up sweet, sugary fruits.

The air smells sweet as berries on bramble bushes begin to ripen.

Hoverflies look like wasps, but they cannot sting.

Huge groups of starlings come together in the evenings. They dip and dive around in the sky looking for somewhere to rest for the night.

A group of starlings is called a murmuration.

Squirrels collect nuts and bury them for winter.

WOODLAND DIARY: JANUARY

In wintertime, the weather gets very cold, and deciduous trees have no leaves left. There is very little food for the animals to eat.

Animals have clever ways to survive the cold and find food in winter.

Squirrels eat the food they stored away before winter.

Birds hop along the ground and nibble up leftover berries.

Wild ponies, like many animals, grow a special, thick winter coat to keep them warm.

Sleepy hedgehogs escape the cold by hibernating in winter. This means that they go into a special kind of sleep—all winter long!

Hedgehogs must eat plenty before winter, so that they can live off their body fat during hibernation.

71

WOODLAND DIARY: APRIL

Spring is a time of new life.
The woodland becomes a busy place!

As the weather gets warmer,
plants push up new shoots from the
ground. Later, beautiful flowers appear.

Trees grow buds that
turn into leaves.

Toads like to keep cool
around wet areas.

The woodland in spring is noisy with birdsong.

Many animals have babies in the spring. Birds' nests are full with eggs and baby chicks.

73

WOODLAND DIARY: JULY

In warm, sunny summer, leafy trees make lots of shade on the forest floor.

Summer is a busy time for insects.

Wasps' nests hang from tree branches.

Beautiful butterflies flutter from flower to flower.

Buzzing bees collect a type of sweet juice called nectar from inside flowers. They bring it back to the nest to feed to other bees.

Spiders make the most of all the summer insects. They spin sticky webs to catch them for their dinner!

AN UNDERGROUND WORLD

Below the surface of the woodland floor, there is a lot of activity.

Burrowers such as rabbits and badgers build their homes in the earth. A rabbit's burrow is called a warren.

A warren is a safe place for rabbits to hide from animals that hunt them, such as foxes.

A badger's burrow is called a sett.
A sett is made up of joined together tunnels.

The tunnels lead to rooms that
are used for sleeping, storing food,
or nesting with babies.

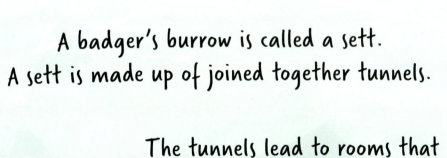

Badgers build setts
by digging with their
long, powerful claws.

Rabbits and badgers spend
lots of time building and
caring for their homes.

WOODLAND RIVER CREATURES

Lots of different creatures live alongside the rivers that wind through woodlands.

Birds such as common sandpipers and oystercatchers search for food on the riverbanks.

River otters eat all kinds of prey, from fish and worms, to birds, eggs, and even frogs.

River otters are built for swimming—their smooth bodies help them move through the water easily.

Baby otters are called pups.

Otters can live both on land and in water.

BUSY AS A BEAVER

Beavers like to live around fresh running water, surrounded by woodland.

Beavers build dams to slow down the flow of the river and make ponds of still water.

They then build lodges in the ponds to live in and keep safe from predators.

Inside the lodges are special rooms for sleeping and for eating.

Large teeth help beavers bite at trees and split them into smaller branches.

Beavers eat plants, bark, twigs, and leaves.

THE SALMON RUN

Every year, salmon go on an incredible journey which often ends in forest rivers.

After spending time at sea, millions of salmon swim up rivers. They lay eggs in the very same place they were born!

In the rivers of North America, large grizzly bears gather to hunt the salmon that swim past.

Overhead, bald eagles circle, waiting for their chance to dive and catch salmon.

Bears use their long claws to hook salmon out of the water.

SCALY AND SLITHERING

Some reptiles live in woodlands, but they are shy, so we don't often see them.

Lizards love to bask in the sun to soak up its warmth.

Some snakes nest in a hole in the ground. Others lay their eggs in warm, rotting leaf litter.

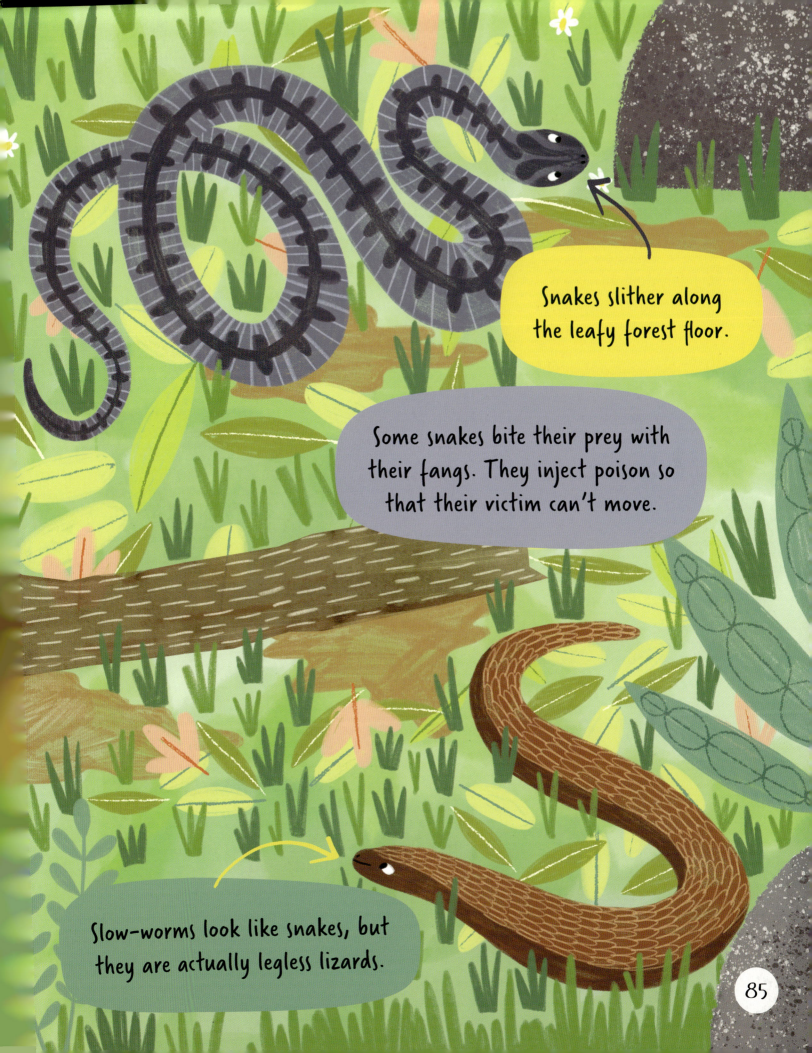

Snakes slither along the leafy forest floor.

Some snakes bite their prey with their fangs. They inject poison so that their victim can't move.

Slow-worms look like snakes, but they are actually legless lizards.

SHOW-OFFS

Many woodland creatures fight and show off to impress each other. This is their way of finding a mate.

A rut is when the leading male deer gathers together the females in his herd.

Younger males challenge him to see who is the strongest.

They roar and toss their heads, crashing their antlers together. Whoever wins the battle is the new leading male.

Up in the sky, buzzards try to attract a mate. They do a soaring, looping dance through the air.

Pairs of emperor dragonflies come together to dance in the air.

WOODLAND ANIMALS QUIZ

How well do you remember facts about woodland animals?
Decide if these sentences are true or false, then check your
answers on page 256.

1 A deciduous forest stays green all year round.

2 Beavers live in homes called setts.

3 Wolves hunt together in packs.

4 Eagles have sharp claws called talons.

5 Grizzly bears eat salmon.

6 Baby otters are called pups.

7 Squirrels build nests called dreys.

8 Trees in a coniferous forest change from season to season.

OUR WORLD

WHAT IS PLANET EARTH?

Our wonderful home planet is called Earth. It travels around the Sun once each year. Every single day, Earth spins around once. The side facing the Sun has daylight.

THE INTERNATIONAL SPACE STATION

On Earth, we have food to eat, air to breathe, sunlight to give us light and heat, and water to drink.

Inside Earth, there are layers of hard and soft metal and rock.

On the surface are the continents, land, and oceans.

Almost 8 billion (8,000,000,000) people live on Earth!

Around Earth is the atmosphere—a blanket of gases that protects the planet.

INSIDE EARTH

Deep in the middle of Earth is the hard, inner core. It is made of metals called iron and nickel.

It is very hot in the inner core—as hot as the surface of the Sun!

INNER CORE

OUTER CORE

The outer core is also made of iron and nickel, but here they are in a soft, melted form.

The next layer is called the mantle, and it makes up much of the planet.

CRUST

UPPER MANTLE

LOWER MANTLE

INNER CORE

OUTER CORE

LOWER MANTLE

UPPER MANTLE

CRUST

The crust is the thinnest layer. It is like a shell around the other layers.

NORTH AMERICA

PACIFIC OCEAN

WORLD MAP

On Earth there are oceans, seas, rivers, lakes—and seven areas of land called continents.

Humans live all over the world on land—in villages, towns, and cities.

SOUTH AMERICA

ATLANTIC OCEAN

The seas and oceans cover more than half of the planet!

ARCTIC OCEAN

We speak different languages depending on where we live. The most common language is Mandarin Chinese.

EUROPE

ASIA

We are able to live in hot deserts, wet rainforests and even icy polar lands.

AFRICA

OCEANIA

INDIAN OCEAN

People live in areas of extreme weather— even in the icy Arctic!

ANTARCTICA

VOLCANOES

When a volcano erupts, hot melted rock bubbles up from deep under ground and bursts out of a mountain as lava.

It pours over the land around the volcano, destroying whatever it meets.

Volcanoes can also be found under the sea, sometimes forming islands.

Hot rocks sometimes shoot out of erupting volcanoes.

Some volcanoes are extinct, which means that they probably won't ever erupt again.

EARTHQUAKES

In Earth's crust, enormous rocks called tectonic plates, move and push against each other.

This causes earthquakes—the ground on Earth's surface shakes.

Some earthquakes are quite small and we can't feel them.

Others are very strong and cause buildings and trees to fall down.

If you live in a place where earthquakes happen often, you have to learn how to stay safe.

If an earthquake happens at sea, this can cause huge waves big enough to destroy houses.

There are some places on Earth where earthquakes happen often, such as the Mid-Atlantic Ridge, shown in this picture.

THE WATER CYCLE

The water cycle is the way that water moves around Earth.

RAIN

SNOW

Humans, animals, and plants need the water cycle to survive.

Most of Earth's water is in the oceans, though some is found in snow and icy glaciers.

Lots of the water goes back to the oceans via rivers, while some stays as water on the ground.

RIVER

The water eventually falls down to Earth as rain, snow, or hail.

These droplets float up into the air. High up in the atmosphere, they form clouds.

EVAPORATION

OCEAN

The Sun heats up the ocean water, and it becomes tiny droplets. This is called evaporation.

RAIN, WIND, AND CLOUDS

Every day when we go outside, we experience the weather.

Experts study special weather maps, so that they can tell what is coming. They look for features such as the wind and types of clouds.

Huge, heavy clouds may bring lots of rain or even thunderstorms.

Low, blanket-like clouds may mean lots of drizzle.

A weather expert is called a meteorologist.

The weather is always changing, depending on what is happening in Earth's atmosphere.

Wispy clouds usually mean mild weather.

WILD WEATHER

Some kinds of weather are wild and even dangerous.

A lightning storm happens when small, frozen raindrops bump into each other inside a thundercloud, making electricity. This then jumps to the ground with a flash.

Hold on tight! A hurricane is a huge tropical storm, with seriously strong winds.

It circles around an "eye" (the middle), where it is strangely calm.

Tornadoes are very powerful winds that spin around in a circle.

Hail is made inside huge clouds during thunderstorms, often on hot days. The balls of ice can cause lots of damage.

105

MOUNTAINS

Mountains are formed over many millions of years.

Some are made when volcanoes erupt over and over, and lava builds up as it cools and becomes hard.

Others are made when two of Earth's underground tectonic plates push up against each other.

Some mountains get lots of snow and have avalanches (when piles of snow fall quickly down a slope).

Mountain habitats are home to many amazing animals, including rare golden eagles.

Lots of people live near mountains, and the natural beauty brings many visitors.

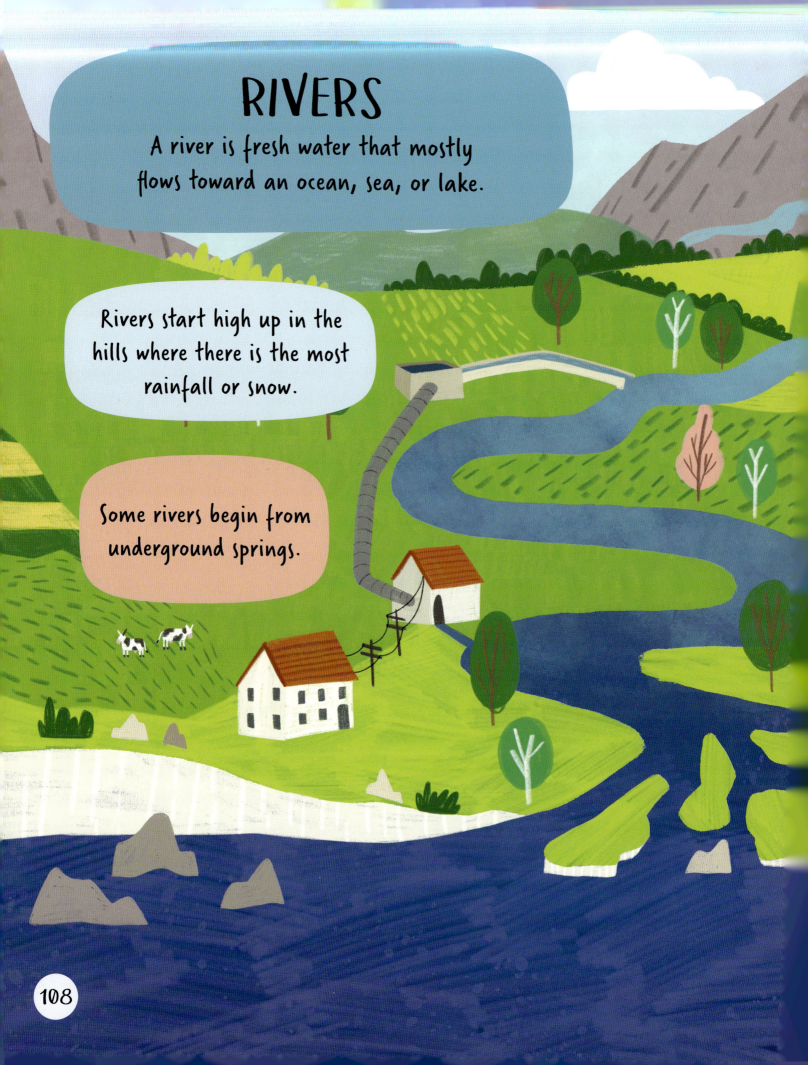

RIVERS

A river is fresh water that mostly flows toward an ocean, sea, or lake.

Rivers start high up in the hills where there is the most rainfall or snow.

Some rivers begin from underground springs.

The start of a river is called its source.

The water flows downhill and follows the shape of the land until it reaches the ocean.

Many animals live near rivers. Some seabirds live where the river meets the ocean.

Humans have lived near rivers for thousands of years. The land nearby is perfect for farming. We also use rivers to take things from one place to another on boats.

RAIN FOREST

Rain forests are very special jungle habitats.

They are home to a huge number of amazing animals and plants.

The weather here is hot and damp. Rain forests get huge amounts of rainfall each year.

People live in rain forests, too, including the Huli tribe of Papua New Guinea.

This tribe is very traditional. They hunt and grow their own food.

Rain forests are sometimes called the lungs of the planet. They produce oxygen—the air that we breathe.

DESERTS

Deserts are very dry areas of land with very little rain. Some are extremely hot, while some are very cold.

The lack of water makes it difficult for plants and animals to live in deserts, but many still do.

People—such as the Bedouin tribe—often live in deserts. They travel from place to place and don't stay in one location for too long.

Even freezing cold Antarctica is a desert—because there is not much rainfall there at all.

Deserts can be found all over the world, from the Sahara in Africa to the Gobi Desert in Asia.

Animals such as camels can go for long periods of time without water, so they live in deserts easily.

113

NORTH AND SOUTH POLES

The North Pole is at the very top part of Earth.

There is no land here, only thick ice and snow.

NORTH POLE

The South Pole is at the very bottom part of Earth.

SOUTH POLE

Around the North Pole is an area of land known as the Arctic.

The Inuit people live in the Arctic. They make homes from ice and snow during winter months.

The area around it is called the Antarctic—it is one of Earth's seven continents.

Scientists and explorers visit the South Pole. They study the land and the wildlife.

115

UNDER THE SEA

Oceans and seas take up much of planet Earth.

Coral reefs are found close to the edges of islands, in warm waters.

These habitats are home to many kinds of fish, such as parrotfish.

Hammerhead sharks live in these waters, searching for food.

The coral is alive! It is made up of tiny little animals with a hard, outer skeleton.

Coral is very delicate, and we must look after it by keeping the water clean. We must not touch it if we get up close.

117

SEASHORE

Seashores are found where the land ends and the sea begins.

Sometimes seashores are rocky and covered in pebbles. Other times they are sandy.

At high tide, the beach is covered with water. At low tide, the water is far out to sea.

At some seashores, there are rocky cliffs. Over time, the waves can wear away the rock to form arches.

When the tide comes in, seawater fills up small pools called rock pools. These are great places to spot seashore life.

Starfish, mussels, and crabs live in these sheltered places.

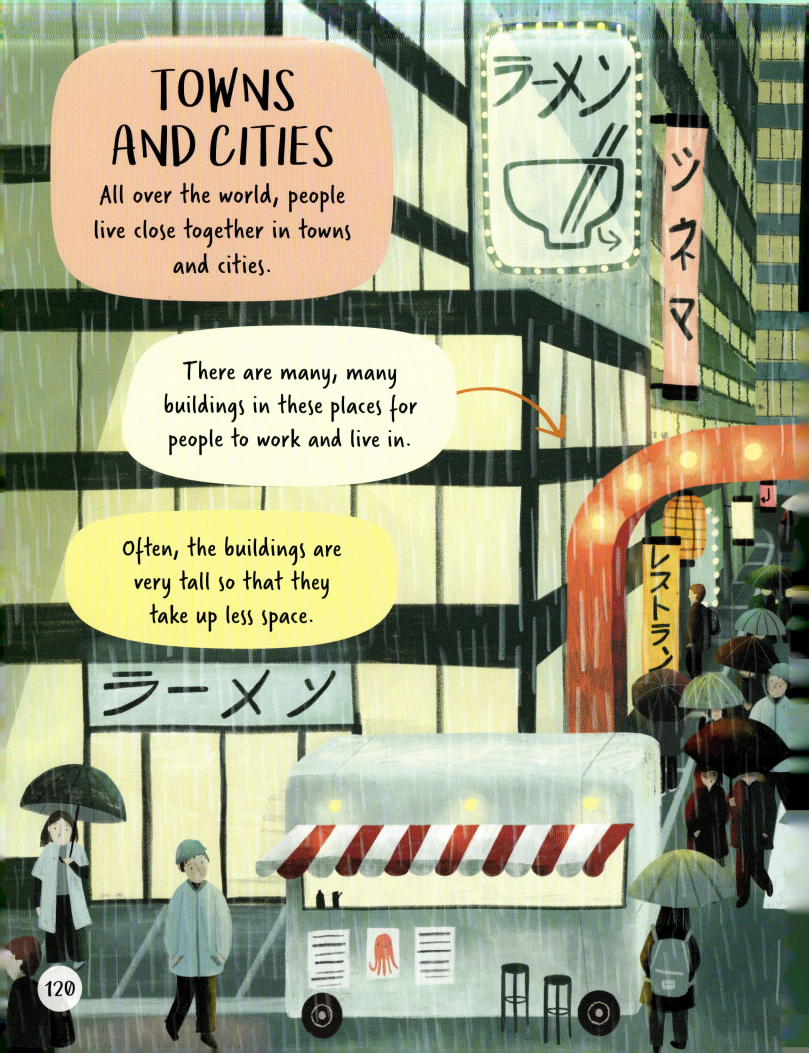

TOWNS AND CITIES

All over the world, people live close together in towns and cities.

There are many, many buildings in these places for people to work and live in.

Often, the buildings are very tall so that they take up less space.

ラーメン

ラーメン

シネマ

レストラン

120

Lots of the buildings are homes, shops, schools, hospitals, and offices.

There are also places to go for fun, such as museums, restaurants, and arcades.

Tokyo in Japan is a very busy city. It is known for its bright lights and amazing technology.

Large towns and cities often have problems with car fumes and waste.

THE FUTURE OF THE PLANET

The nature on planet Earth gives us the food, air, and water we need to live, so it is important that we look after Earth in return.

Many animals, including bees and butterflies, spread seeds from flower to flower. This helps plants grow into new ones.

We need lots of plants to live because they give us food, and they make the air that we breathe.

Plants and animals need their own places to live and grow. We can all play a part in keeping those places clean and healthy.

Some waste can be harmful to plants and animals. Recycling waste whenever possible will help protect our wildlife.

OUR WORLD QUIZ

How well do you remember facts about our world?
Decide if these sentences are true or false, then check
your answers on page 256.

1 The start of a river is called its source.

2 The Earth travels around the Sun once each year.

3 It is very cold in Earth's inner core.

4 The seas and oceans cover less than half of the planet.

5 The most common language is Mandarin Chinese.

6 A volcano that is extinct will definitely erupt again.

7 Evaporation happens when the sun heats up water.

8 Mountains are formed very quickly, in just a few minutes.

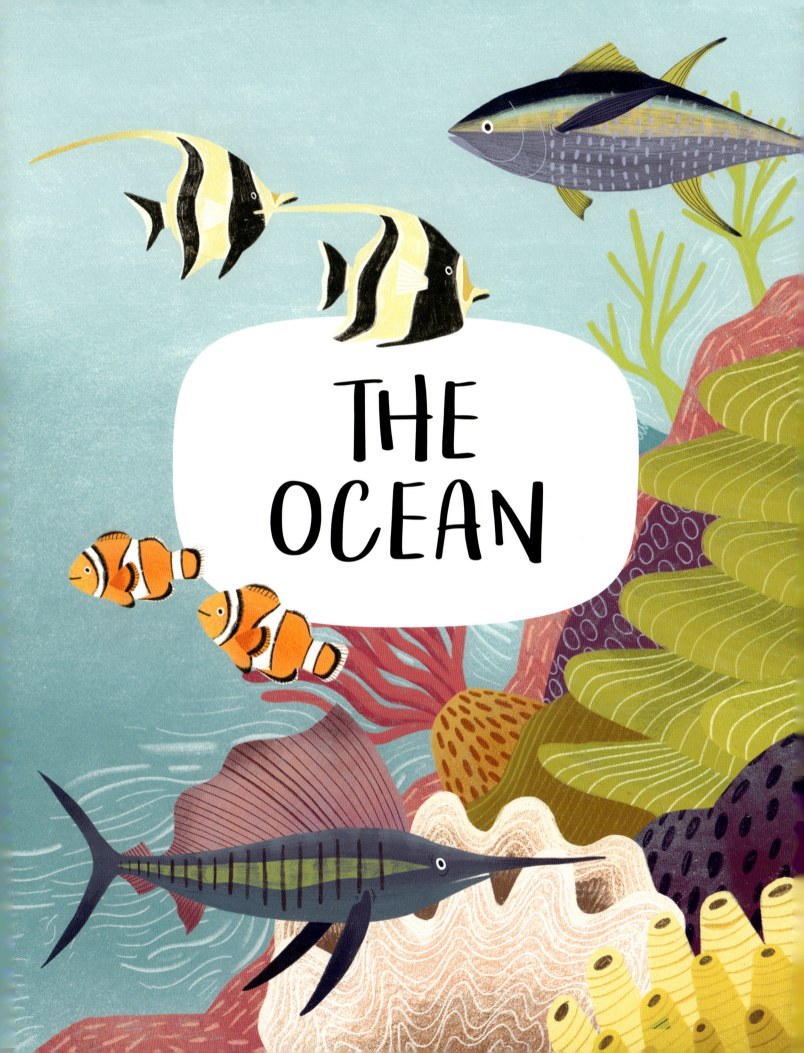

THE
OCEAN

OUR WATERY WORLD

More than two-thirds of our planet is covered with water. The world's oceans are home to millions of plants and animals.

An ocean is a very large area of salty water.

The coast is where the land meets the sea. Lots of plants and animals live here.

The sea moves in and out of the shore twice every day. We call this the tide.

Different sea creatures are adapted (suited) to live in different ocean environments.

Ocean water is always on the move—it flows around Earth in patterns called currents.

Most sea creatures live near the surface of the ocean, where it's warmer.

Oceans are warm or cold in different places around the world. The Arctic and the Southern oceans are the coldest. The Indian Ocean is the warmest.

The Five Oceans of the World

Arctic Ocean

Atlantic Ocean

Pacific Ocean

Indian Ocean

Southern Ocean

IN A ROCK POOL

When the tide goes out, small pools of water collect between the rocks on the shore.

Rock pools are warmer and saltier than the rest of the sea. Plants and animals are adapted to live in them.

Crabs scuttle in and out of rock pools. Their hard shells protect them from crashing waves and predators.

Anemones wave their tentacles in the water, catching food that drifts by.

Starfish have lots of tiny feet on the underside of their arms. They use them to walk on the seabed.

Seaweed, such as bladderwrack, attaches to rocks. It grows in long strands.

Shrimp swim near the bottom. Their bodies blend in with their surroundings.

Limpets stick their shells firmly onto dry rock. They move around under water, eating algae.

AWESOME OTTERS

Sea otters are mammals. They live along
the coasts of North America and Asia.

Sea otters live in groups,
sometimes holding paws
to stay together.

They float on their backs
at the surface. A sea otter
pup (baby) lies on its
mother's tummy.

Their thick fur
keeps them warm
and dry. Their
webbed feet help
them swim.

A sea otter puts a rock on its chest and bashes a clam against it. When the shell breaks, the otter eats the insides.

They dive under water to hunt for sea creatures, such as crabs and clams.

Sometimes they wrap themselves in kelp (a type of seaweed), so that they don't float away while they sleep.

131

AMAZING PELICANS

Pelicans are famous for their huge beak pouches, which they use to scoop up fish from the ocean.

A pelican's pouch can hold three times more water than its stomach can.

Pelicans are very large birds. Their wingspan measures more than the height of a man.

When brown pelicans hunt, they fly over the surface then dive head-first into the water.

A pelican's throat pouch is called a gular.

The pelican scoops up the fish in the water. The water drains out of its beak, then the pelican swallows the fish whole.

Pelicans have large, webbed feet. They keep their eggs warm by standing on them!

133

SUPER SHARKS

These ancient fish have existed for around 300 million years. Sharks live in every ocean on Earth.

There are about 300 different species (type) of shark.

Sharks can have hundreds of teeth, arranged in rows. When a tooth falls out, another moves forward to take its place.

Hammerhead sharks have wide, flattened heads. Their wide-set eyes scan the ocean for prey.

Sharks can sense tiny electric currents in the water. This helps them find food and avoid predators.

A tiger shark is even longer than a family car.

Tiger sharks will eat almost any other creature they can catch. This includes seals, fish, turtles, birds, and even other sharks!

A CORAL REEF

Many bright and beautiful creatures make their home in the warm waters of a coral reef. The largest coral reef is the Great Barrier Reef in Australia.

Humphead wrasse fish are longer than a man. They eat sea urchins, fish, and coral.

There are hundreds of different kinds of coral.

Sea fan

Brain coral

Each coral is a group of tiny creatures called polyps. The polyps make hard layers that form reefs over many years.

Reef fish called moorish idols often swim in pairs.

Like other reptiles, sea snakes come to the surface to breathe air. They attack prey with a venomous bite.

Table coral

Sea anemones catch prey with stinging tentacles. Clownfish do not feel the stings, so they can use anemones to hide in.

Bright, patterned sea slugs crawl along the bottom of the reef.

Giant clam

PECULIAR PORCUPINEFISH

Some ocean creatures have clever ways to protect themselves from enemies.

Porcupinefish are able to puff themselves up like a balloon. They become two or three times their usual size.

Porcupinefish get their name from the sharp spines all over their bodies.

When porcupinefish puff themselves up, they look like a spiky ball. Predators think twice before attacking such an uncomfortable meal!

Porcupinefish are found in warm and shallow waters in the Indian, Pacific, and Atlantic oceans.

There are around 90 different species (type) of porcupinefish.

If that doesn't put off attackers, porcupinefish have another way to defend themselves—they are highly poisonous to eat.

CLEVER OCTOPUSES

These curious creatures have some very useful tricks.

Their eight long tentacles, called arms, have suckers all along them. These help octopuses to catch hold of crabs and lobsters to eat.

Octopuses have a large donut-shaped brain. They also have a minibrain in each of the eight arms!

As well as their nine "brains," octopuses also have three hearts and blue blood!

Octopuses squirt out a cloud of ink to confuse attackers. Then they swim away fast!

Octopuses have the ability to change their skin tone to blend in with their surroundings.

To fool predators, mimic octopuses change their body shape and pretend to be other creatures, such as venomous sea snakes.

Some octopuses use old shells as cunning hiding places.

MAGICAL SEAHORSES

These strange and beautiful fish live in shallow waters and coral reefs.

Seahorses are fish. Instead of scales, they have bony plates on their bodies.

Seahorses swim upright. They eat by sucking tiny sea creatures and algae through their long snouts.

Most seahorses are small, but a pygmy seahorse is tiny enough to fit on your fingernail!

Seahorses do not have a stomach. They have to eat nearly all the time, because food passes through their bodies so quickly.

They use their long, curled tails to hold on to plants or coral.

Male seahorses, rather than female, give birth to young.

GENTLE DUGONGS

These shy mammals spend most of their time on the seabed, munching on seagrass.

Because they are mammals, dugongs need to come to the surface to breathe air. They can hold their breath under water for 11 minutes.

Dugongs live in the warm, coastal waters of the Indian and Pacific oceans.

Sometimes dugongs will "stand" on their tails and poke their noses out of the water to take a breath!

Although they spend most of their time alone or in pairs, dugongs can gather together in huge herds of 100.

Dugongs have really good hearing. They squeak and chirp to each other.

Strange as it may seem, dugongs are related to elephants!

145

SPEEDY SWIMMERS

Out in the open ocean, creatures often use speed
to catch prey—or to avoid predators.

They have a long spike, or bill, above their mouth. Sailfish use their bill like a spear to attack fish to eat.

Sailfish get their name from the large, sail-like fin that runs along their back.

Sailfish are the fastest fish in the sea!

With their streamlined bodies, tuna are built for speed.

To escape predators such as tuna, flying fish swim really fast. Then they flap their tails to leap out of the sea.

Flying fish spread out their fins, like wings. They can glide through the air for about 45 seconds.

In its lifetime, a sailfish will swim the equivalent of eight times around the world!

ADVENTUROUS TURTLES

These beautiful reptiles live in warm seas all over the world.

A tough shell helps to protect sea turtles from predators.

They use their sharp beaklike mouth to eat creatures such as jellyfish and sea sponges.

There are seven different species (types) of sea turtle. The largest is the leatherback. It is much bigger than a person.

A female turtle will swim hundreds of miles to the beach where she hatched. This is where she lays her own eggs.

Baby turtles are called hatchlings. They crawl to the sea, trying to avoid predators, such as birds.

Sea turtles can hold their breath under water for hours!

149

ADORABLE DOLPHINS

Bottlenose dolphins have powerful fins that make them speedy swimmers.

Baby dolphins can swim just minutes after they are born. They stay close to their mothers for around six years.

Living together in pods (groups) gives dolphins protection from enemies. It also allows them to hunt for food as a team.

Bottlenose dolphins live in warm waters.

Like whales, dolphins come to the surface to breathe air through their blowholes—then dive back below the waves.

Dolphins click, squeak, and even bump heads to send messages to each other. They are very clever creatures.

MYSTERIOUS RAYS

With their wide, flattened bodies and long, thin tails, rays are unusual-looking fish.

Giant manta rays can travel long distances across the open ocean. They sometimes leap out of the water!

Rays live in many of the world's oceans. Most live on the bottom of shallow seas.

Giant mantas can measure as wide as four people lying end to end!

Mantas flap their fins like wings to "fly" through the water.

The large flaps on either side of a manta's head are used to push plankton into their mouths.

Electric rays can deliver a powerful electric shock. They use this to attack prey and to defend themselves.

153

INTO THE DEEP

As the ocean gets deeper, it also gets colder and darker. Strange creatures live down here.

Plants cannot grow in the deepest parts of the ocean. Creatures that live here eat pieces of food that drift down from above—or each other.

Viperfish have large mouths with long, sharp teeth. Their bodies can make their own light.

The Mariana Trench is at the bottom of the Pacific Ocean. Its deepest point is greater than the height of Mount Everest!

Goblin sharks use electricity to find food in the dark. Their jaws shoot out of their mouth to grab hold of prey.

Anglerfish have a spine on their head called a lure. The lure glows in the dark, attracting prey to swim close.

Black swallower fish have super-stretchy stomachs. They can gulp down creatures double their own size!

Tripod fish use their three long, bony spines to "stand" on the seafloor, waiting for tiny creatures to swim by.

WONDERFUL WHALES

Blue whales live in every ocean on Earth.
They are the gentle giants of the sea.

Heavier than any of the dinosaurs, blue whales are the largest animals alive on Earth today.

Krill are tiny shrimplike creatures. They gather in huge groups called swarms. The swarms look like pink clouds in the water and can contain millions of krill.

Imagine 17 people swimming in a line … that's how long a blue whale is!

Instead of teeth, blue whales have baleen plates, which look a little bit like combs. The baleen plates filter (strain) krill from the water.

Blue whales eat around four million krill every day.

These massive mammals can hold their breath under water for over an hour.

BEAUTIFUL JELLYFISH

Jellyfish are found in every ocean on Earth. Some prefer warm seas, while others live in deep, cold waters.

Jellyfish are invertebrates, which means that they have no backbone. They also have no brain!

A large group of jellyfish is called a bloom.

Many jellyfish, such as these mauve stingers, are bioluminescent. This means that they can make light in their bodies.

These jellyfish have long, stinging tentacles that they use to catch fish and tiny sea creatures to eat.

Jellyfish can be dangerous. Some types of jellyfish are more venomous than any snake and can kill a human.

The largest jellyfish can grow bigger than a person. The tiniest can be smaller than your fingernail!

ICY-COLD WATERS

At the very top of Earth lies the chilly Arctic Ocean. In the winter, most of the ocean is covered with ice.

Seals and walruses have a thick layer of fat under their skin, called blubber. This keeps them warm in the frozen Arctic.

Seals dive deep under the ice in search of Arctic cod.

Narwhals are a type of whale. Male narwhals have a long, spiral tusk.

Hungry polar bears wait for seals to come up for air.

Walruses use their long tusks to dig for shellfish on the seabed—and to fight other walruses.

Killer whales, or orcas, are a type of dolphin. They hunt seals in groups called pods.

GIANT SQUID

Lurking in the ocean depths is a real-life sea monster.

Longer than a bus, giant and colossal squid are the biggest invertebrates in the world.

The only known predators of giant squid are sperm whales. Many sperm whales have scars caused by giant squid suckers.

Giant squid eat fish and smaller squid. Their sharp beaks rip food apart.

A giant squid's eyes are bigger than soccer balls! Good eyesight helps the squid scan the ocean for food—and predators.

Giant squid have eight long arms and two tentacles with suckers. The suckers help them grab hold of prey.

INCREDIBLE PENGUINS

These birds cannot fly, but they are great swimmers and divers.

Penguins are found only in the southern part of the world. These emperor penguins live in Antarctica, the coldest place on Earth.

Emperor penguins slide on their bellies across the ice and into the water. They dive deep down to search for fish and squid to eat.

Penguins live in large groups, called colonies.

In the freezing Antarctic winter, emperor penguins huddle together to keep warm.

Their feathers are covered with a special oil. This keeps penguins warm and dry in the cold water.

Emperor penguins can dive deeper than any other bird and can hold their breath for over half an hour.

OCEAN ANIMALS QUIZ

How well do you remember facts about ocean creatures? Decide if these sentences are true or false, then check your answers on page 256.

1 An ocean is a very large area of salty water.

2 Sea otters live on their own.

3 Tiger sharks are tiny.

4 Clownfish hide in sea anemones.

5 Porcupine fish are safe to eat.

6 Male seahorses give birth to young.

7 Sailfish are the slowest fish.

8 Blue whales are heavier than any of the dinosaurs.

SPACE

STARRY NIGHT

Look up! There are so many stars in the sky. No one could count them all. It would take too long!

The stars look like tiny, twinkling dots of light.

If you connect the starry dots into groups, you can make pictures, such as a bear or a swan.

Look through a telescope, and stars will seem bigger and brighter.

A star is a very big, very hot ball of gas. The gas is burning fiercely, and that makes the star very bright.

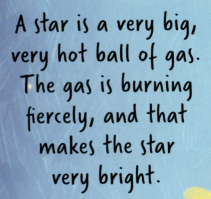

The Sun is a star, but it looks different from other stars because it is closer to us.

Stars are very, very far away. It would take thousands of years to travel to the nearest one.

Some stars are billions of years old. That's an awful lot of birthdays!

169

THE STARS ABOVE US

Our nearest star, the Sun, is just one of many billions of stars that make up the Milky Way. The Milky Way is a group of stars, called a galaxy.

On a very clear night, we can see this beautiful blanket of stars spread across the sky.

Ancient Romans called it the "road of milk," and ancient Greeks named it the "milky circle."

For a long time, people thought that ALL the stars were in the Milky Way, but we now know there are many, many more galaxies filled with all kinds of different stars.

Constellations are star patterns in the sky. You can use star maps to find them.

Orion is one of the most famous constellations. It can be seen throughout the whole world.

Earth is here

Constellations are useful because they help us recognize and find certain stars, for example, the North Star, which explorers used to find their way.

WHAT IS THE UNIVERSE?

When we look up into space, we are looking out into the Universe. It's billions of years old!

The Universe is EVERYTHING, including all the stars and planets and things we can see. It also includes all the things we can't see.

The Universe is growing outward, getting bigger all the time.

The Big Bang is the name experts use to describe the moment the Universe first formed in a huge explosion.

Scientists are trying to understand where we are in the Universe— are we on the edge or in the middle?

THE SOLAR SYSTEM

The solar system is a moving system of planets, moons, and other space objects.

Asteroid belt

Earth

Earth, like Mercury, Venus, and Mars, is a rocky planet.

Venus

Mercury

SUN

The Sun is in the middle of the solar system.

The Sun pulls the solar system's planets toward it. This keeps the planets from zooming off into outer space.

Jupiter

The planets travel around the Sun on paths called orbits.

Neptune

Uranus

The orbits are different shapes and distances from the Sun, depending on the planet.

Jupiter, Saturn, Uranus, and Neptune are mostly made up of gases, which means we can't land on their surface.

Mars

Saturn

HOW BiG?

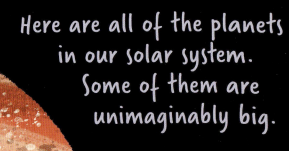

Here are all of the planets in our solar system. Some of them are unimaginably big.

← Jupiter

Jupiter is the biggest planet.

Saturn

You could fit 1,321 planets the size of Earth inside Saturn.

176

Uranus

Neptune

The Sun is by far the biggest object in our solar system—it's nearly 10 times wider than the next biggest!

Moon

Earth

SUN

The four closest planets to the Sun (Mercury, Venus, Earth, and Mars) are the four smallest planets, too.

Mars

Venus

Mercury is the smallest planet and the closest to the Sun.

Mercury

OUR LIFE-GIVING STAR

The Sun, our closest star, is an enormous ball of burning hot gas in space.

One of the main reasons we have life on Earth is the Sun—it gives us light and warmth.

The hot gas in the Sun is always moving. Solar flares are sudden bright flashes on the Sun's surface.

Scientists study the Sun to discover how it works and to understand more about other stars, too.

More than one million planet Earths would fit inside the Sun. It's enormous!

MERCURY: THE WRINKLY PLANET

The closest planet to the Sun, Mercury is the smallest planet in our solar system and is only a little bigger than Earth's Moon.

Mercury moves around the Sun very quickly. One year on the planet lasts the same amount of time as roughly 3 months on Earth.

It is named after the Roman god Mercury, a messenger who could travel at very fast speeds.

This planet looks as though it has wrinkles, but it is, in fact, covered with large ridges called scarps.

These scarps were formed as Mercury's core cooled, causing the planet to shrink.

Mercury is also covered in craters (huge dents caused by crashing space rocks).

One of the craters is named after a famous painter, Vincent Van Gogh.

Experts believe that ice may possibly exist inside the planet's craters.

VENUS: OUR SISTER PLANET

Venus, the second planet from the Sun, is also known as our sister planet.

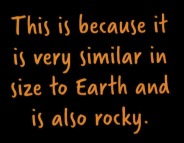

This is because it is very similar in size to Earth and is also rocky.

Venus is much hotter than Earth, which means that humans could never live there.

It also has a thick, toxic atmosphere. This means that the layer of gases that covers the planet would be deadly for us to breathe.

It can be seen from Earth on a clear night, as its surface is lit up so brightly by the Sun.

Venus stands out in the night sky because its light is steady, not twinkly like the stars. Can you spot it?

One day on Venus is very long—the same as 243 Earth days!

Venus is named after the Roman goddess of love and beauty.

The Earth gives us air to breathe and a protective layer of gas that covers the planet like a blanket. The Sun gives us light and heat.

Nearly three-quarters of Earth's surface is covered in water.

From snow-capped mountains and sun-drenched deserts, to bright coral reefs and green rain forests—life on Earth is beautiful.

Our seas, rivers, and lakes are full of life. If our oceans are healthy, it helps keep our planet healthy.

EARTH: OUR PLACE IN SPACE

The largest rocky planet, and third planet from the Sun is our home—planet Earth.

Scientists build amazing machines that can leave Earth and travel into space.

Earth is often called a goldilocks planet because conditions here are "just right" for life to exist.

Satellites travel around and around the Earth. Rockets are vehicles that can carry people to satellites, the Moon, or distant planets!

MOON: LUNAR LIFE

The Moon is a huge ball of space rock.

The Moon is a satellite, a space object that follows a path around a planet—Earth!

Scientists think that the Moon may have formed billions of years ago.

The Moon is the only place in space where humans have actually set foot.

As the Moon travels around Earth, the part of the Moon that faces the Sun is lit up.

Crescent Moon

Full Moon

New Moon

The Moon appears to change shape throughout each month. These changes are called phases.

Each year, the Moon moves a little farther away from us.

Many of the markings, known as craters, on the Moon's surface, can be spotted from Earth.

Other planets have moons, too, but not all. Our Moon is the fifth-largest in our solar system.

187

MARS: THE RED PLANET

The fourth planet from the Sun, Mars is also known as the red planet. Its rocky surface is covered in an orange-red dust.

Named after the Roman god of war, this planet is about half the size of Earth.

Scientists believe that there may be salty water on its surface. Perhaps there was once life on Mars!

Like Earth, Mars is covered in ice at its north and south poles.

It would be very hard for people to live on this freezing-cold planet. However scientists are looking into whether it may be possible for humans to live there in the future.

The highest mountain in the solar system is here—Olympus Mons.

Sometimes we can see Mars glowing in the night sky from Earth.

It is almost three times as high as the highest mountain on Earth.

Special spacecraft called rovers have been to the surface of Mars to send information home. That's one of the ways we know so much about this planet.

189

Jupiter is named after the Roman king of the gods.

The swirls on Jupiter's outer surface look beautiful. However, they would be deadly to breathe.

There are many storms on Jupiter, such as the Great Red Spot. This hurricane is bigger than Earth and has been going for almost 200 years!

JUPITER: THE BIGGEST OF ALL

Jupiter, the fifth planet from the Sun, is the largest planet in our solar system.

It would be impossible to stand on the surface of this great gas giant, because it isn't solid.

Jupiter is more than twice the size of all of the other planets put together.

Jupiter has an incredible 95 moons in its orbit.

The largest of all, Ganymede, is even bigger than Mercury.

SATURN: THE JEWEL OF THE SOLAR SYSTEM

Saturn is the sixth planet from the Sun. It is famous for the many sparkling rings that circle around its middle.

These rings are made up of broken pieces of icy space rock. They were first spotted by famous astronomer Galileo hundreds of years ago.

Saturn is named after the god of farming in ancient Rome.

Of Saturn's 146 moons, Titan is the biggest. It is the second-biggest moon in the entire solar system.

Titan is the only other space object with clouds, like Earth. It has its own atmosphere like a planet.

Like Jupiter, the beautiful planet Saturn is a gas giant.

Saturn is made of gas, so it is very light. If it was placed in a GIANT bowl of water, it would float!

URANUS: THE ICE GIANT

While it very slowly travels around the Sun, Uranus looks like a ball rolling on its side.

Uranus is the seventh planet from the Sun and the third gas giant. Like Saturn, it, too has rings.

Uranus' rings run from its top to its bottom. This makes it look like it has tipped over.

It is made up of different gases to Jupiter and Saturn, and is much more icy.

It was the first planet discovered using a telescope, rather than the naked eye. It was almost named George, after the king of England at the time!

The 28 moons of Uranus are mostly named after characters in plays by the famous playwright, William Shakespeare.

Instead, and more sensibly, it was named after a Greek god of the sky.

One of the most famous moons, Miranda, is covered in icy canyons.

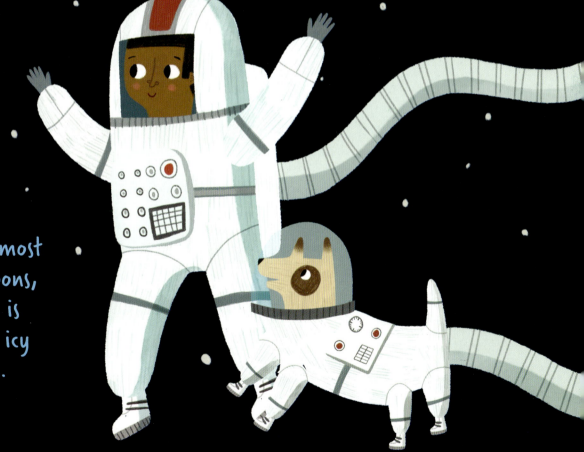

NEPTUNE: THE BLUE PLANET

At the edge of our solar system is Neptune, the eighth planet.
It is also the final gas giant.

It is very windy on Neptune. These winds reach far higher speeds than those on Earth.

Through a telescope,
Neptune glows a
beautiful bright blue.
It is named after the
Roman god of the sea.

Neptune's biggest moon
is Triton. Unusually,
it spins in the opposite
direction to all of
Neptune's other moons.

Neptune has rings running
around its middle, perhaps made
from other smashed-up space
rocks that came too close.

DWARF PLANETS

A dwarf planet is similar to a true planet in many ways.

What makes dwarf planets different is mostly that they are smaller than main planets.

Like the main planets, dwarf planets travel around the Sun in an orbit.

Dysnomia (Eris's moon)

Eris is the farthest dwarf planet from the Sun.

We used to think Pluto was a main planet, but scientists changed their minds and decided it was a dwarf planet instead.

Haumea is found beyond Neptune.

Mysterious Makemake is thought to be the third-largest dwarf planet.

Dwarf planet Ceres is the closest to Earth. It is found in the asteroid belt between Mars and Jupiter.

Experts believe that there could be thousands of dwarf planets.

COMETS, ASTEROIDS, AND METEORS

As well as planets and moons, space is full of different kinds of space rock.

Comets are big pieces of rock and ice that whirl around the Sun.

Behind them, comets trail a tail made of gas. It can be hundreds —or even thousands—of miles long.

Asteroids are pieces of space rock that can be just a few feet in length—or big enough to have their own moons.

Between Mars and Jupiter is a huge band of thousands of asteroids.

Vesta is one of the largest asteroids. It is like a small, rocky planet.

This picture shows how different types of space rock look when viewed from space.

Comet

Earth

Meteors

Asteroid

Meteors are smaller pieces of rock. If they come close to the Earth, they burn up as they fall to the ground. Then, they are known as shooting stars.

SPACE TELESCOPES

Telescopes let us see farther into space than we can see with just our eyes. Some are based on Earth, but some have been sent into space.

Telescopes in space can see farther than telescopes on Earth.

The Hubble Space Telescope showed that in just one small area of space, there were more than 5,500 galaxies.

Galileo invented the first simple telescope more than 400 years ago!

Across Earth today, there are many huge telescopes, such as Keck 1 and Keck 2 on the Island of Hawaii.

These enormous telescopes make distant stars easy to see and study.

The James Webb Space Telescope is a new telescope set to be sent into space. It will be able to take photos farther into space than ever before.

SPACE TRAVEL

To send a spacecraft into space, scientists use a launch vehicle, or rocket.

Rockets have incredibly powerful engines. These help them reach speeds fast enough to leave Earth's atmosphere.

They burn lots of fuel, which gives them enough energy to move.

The Space Shuttle is one of the most famous spacecrafts ever. Now retired, it flew 135 missions and carried seven astronauts each time.

It is easiest to launch craft into space from near the equator, the invisible line around Earth.

The new and improved Space Launch System (SLS) will soon be in use. It may take astronauts to Mars for the first time ever.

The Space Shuttle

One space telescope, Kepler, has been sent out of our solar system to find new planet systems. More and more are discovered all the time!

THE INTERNATIONAL SPACE STATION

Many nations from across the world came together to build this amazing space station.

The International Space Station (ISS) orbits Earth.

Astronauts eat three meals a day. They eat with knives and forks, like we do on Earth. But they don't eat outside the station of course!

The ISS was built so that astronauts could do scientific experiments in space. They look at what happens to our bodies when we are in space, for example.

The ISS is as long as a football stadium. You can sometimes see it zooming across the sky! It looks like a very fast-moving plane.

On the ISS, astronauts have to exercise for two hours each day to stay fit. Otherwise, their muscles and bones would get weak very quickly.

207

SPACE QUIZ

How well do you remember facts about space? Decide if these sentences are true or false, then check your answers on page 256.

1 The ISS is where astronauts do scientific experiments in space.

2 Rockets are used to launch craft into space.

3 A comet is a big piece of rock and ice.

4 Asteroids can be large enough to have their own moons.

5 Haumea is the closest planet to the Sun.

6 Neptune is a bright pink planet.

7 Jupiter is the smallest planet in our solar system.

8 The Great Red Spot is a storm on Jupiter.

HOW THINGS WORK

WHAT MAKES BICYCLES GO?

Bicycles are machines that help us get from one place to another.

BRAKE

HANDLEBARS

The handlebars change the direction of the front wheel.

To stop the bicycle, you squeeze the brakes, and little pads push against the wheels to stop the bicycle.

The pedals are connected to a gear. The back wheel has a gear, too. Both gears are linked by a chain.

GEAR

PEDAL

CHAIN

When you turn the pedals, it drags the chain around which turns the back wheel.

WHEEL

When the back wheel turns, it pushes the bicycle forward and forces the front wheel to turn.

HOW DO SHOES STAY FASTENED?

There are simple but clever inventions we use to fasten our shoes.

Some shoes use laces, others use buckles, and some use hook-and-loop fasteners.

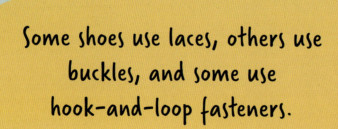

213

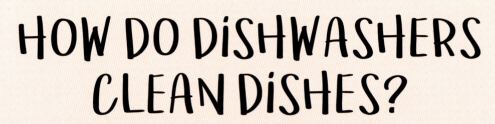

HOW DO DISHWASHERS CLEAN DISHES?

Dishwashers are machines that clean and rinse your dirty dishes.

The dishwasher was invented more than 130 years ago. The first dishwasher worked in a similar way to the ones we use today!

SOAP COMPARTMENT

A pump heats up water and pushes it into the spray arms.

The spray arms turn around, spraying clean water onto the dishes.

Clean water flows in through a pipe.

Dirty water drains away.

SPRAY ARM

PUMP

Dishwashers need electricity and water to work.

A soap compartment pops open during the wash. The soap mixes with the water in the machine.

HOW DOES A SPACECRAFT LAUNCH?

Launch vehicles are used to send spacecraft and satellites into space. They need rocket power to get there.

Rockets help blast the launch vehicle into space. They burn fuel until it runs out. The empty rockets drop back to Earth. Some can be collected and used again.

PAYLOAD FAIRING

MAIN ROCKET

ROCKET BOOSTER

The spacecraft is contained inside a nose cone called the payload fairing.

The fuel in the rockets needs oxygen to burn. We normally find oxygen as a gas in the air.

Inside the rocket, there is liquid oxygen. When it is mixed with fuel in the rocket's combustion chamber, it makes an explosion.

INSIDE MAIN ROCKET

FUEL

LIQUID OXYGEN

COMBUSTION CHAMBER

Waste gases blast out and down from the rocket. This forces the rocket up.

WHAT KEEPS A LOCK LOCKED?

We keep our homes safe by locking the doors.

When you turn the key in a lock, a piece of metal goes in and out. This is called the deadbolt.

Inside the lock there is a set of levers, which let the deadbolt move in and out.

← The key has parts cut out of it in a special pattern.

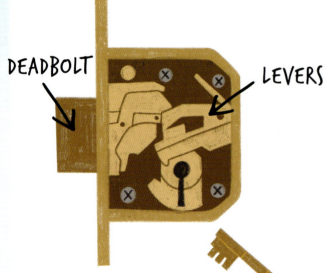

DEADBOLT

LEVERS

As it is turned, each cut-out part on the key lines up with a lever.

When all the levers line up, the deadbolt slides back into the lock.

When the deadbolt is inside the lock, the door can open. When the deadbolt slides into the slot in the door frame, it holds the door in place.

HOW DOES A PHONE MAKE A CALL?

Cellular phones are a handy way to keep in touch with friends and family.

When you talk, a tiny microphone inside the phone picks up your voice and turns the sounds into an electrical signal.

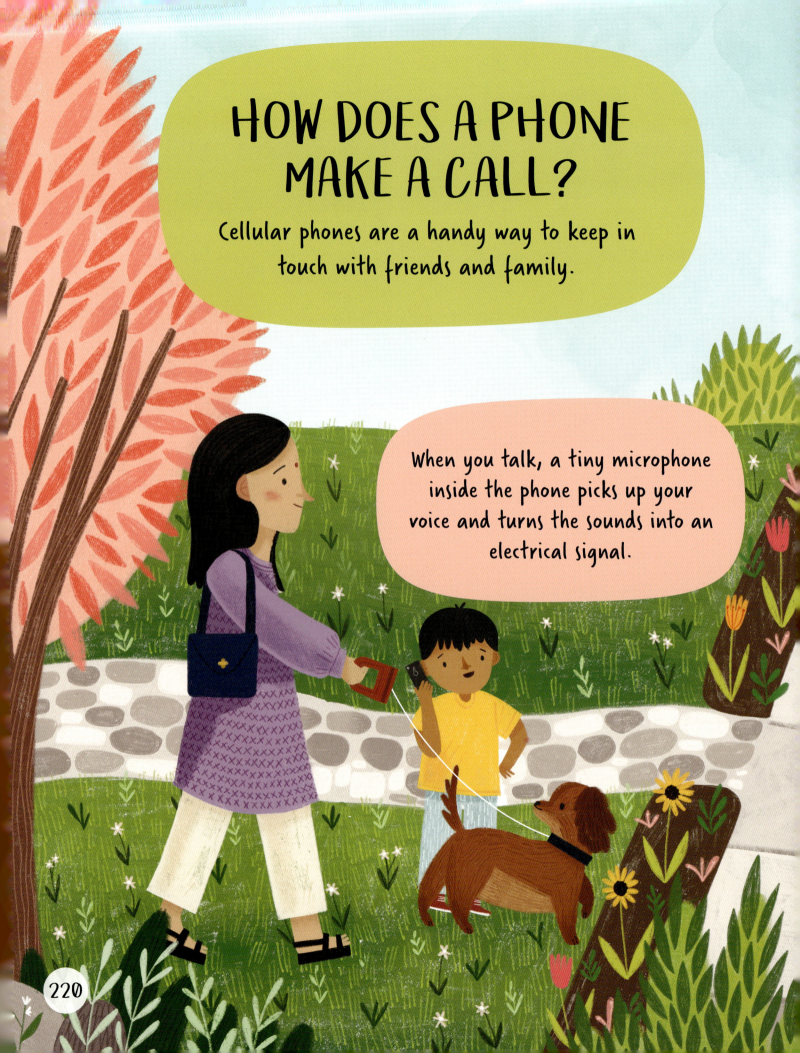

The phone turns the signal into radio waves. Radio waves are invisible waves of energy that can travel through the air and space.

A tall structure at a base station receives the radio waves.

The base station sends the radio waves to a central station in the area.

Their phone receives the radio waves and changes them back into sounds.

The central station sends the radio waves to a base station close to your friend.

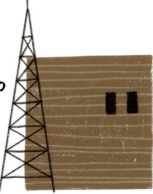

That base station sends the radio waves to their phone.

HOW DOES A VACUUM CLEANER WORK?

A vacuum cleaner sucks up dust and dirt from your floor.

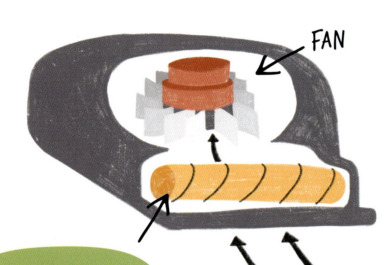

FAN

When you turn the vacuum cleaner on, the motor makes a fan spin very fast.

A rotating (spinning) brush at the front loosens all the dust and dirt from the floor.

The fan spins so quickly that it sucks in air, dust, and dirt.

The filter traps small particles of dust while larger particles spin around inside the container.

Clean air flows out.

Dirty air is sucked up by the fan through a pipe and into the container.

When the container is full of dust and dirt, it is emptied, ready for next time.

Some vacuum cleaners have bags that the dirt goes into, and some have see-through containers. But they all work in the same way!

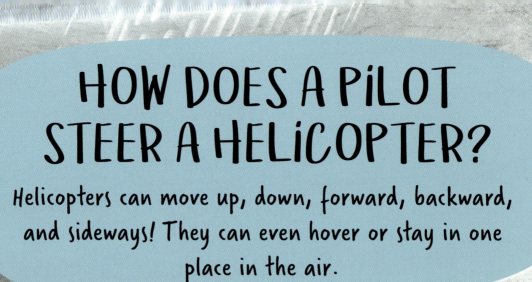

HOW DOES A PILOT STEER A HELICOPTER?

Helicopters can move up, down, forward, backward, and sideways! They can even hover or stay in one place in the air.

Helicopters are very useful in an emergency, because they can fly almost anywhere.

ROTOR BLADE

The engine turns the rotor blades really fast to lift the helicopter into the air.

A smaller tail rotor keeps the helicopter from spinning around in circles.

The main rotor blades are connected to the swash plate. The pilot tilts the swash plate, which makes the rotors tilt.

SWASH PLATE

When the rotors tilt forward, the helicopter moves forward. When they tilt back, the helicopter moves backward.

Each rotor blade is shaped so that the air flows over the top of it quickly.

225

HOW DO PENS MAKE MARKS?

Hundreds of years ago, people wrote and drew pictures using the tip of a feather dipped in ink. It was very messy!

Ballpoint pens were invented in the 1930s.

A ballpoint pen has a thin plastic tube inside. The tube is filled with quick-drying ink.

The tip of a ballpoint pen contains a tiny ball.

As you push the pen across paper, the ball rolls around and gets coated with ink. The pen leaves a line of ink on the paper.

The nib (tip) of a felt-tip pen is made from nylon. The nib soaks up ink from the main part of the pen.

227

HOW DOES A COMPUTER WORK?

A computer, such as a laptop or tablet, is a machine that follows a set of instructions. It makes calculations and stores information.

The parts of a computer you can touch are called hardware.

Information goes into the computer through the keyboard, mouse, camera, or touchscreen.

A program is a set of instructions a computer follows to complete a task. Together, programs are called software.

This is the screen. Screens, printers, and speakers are called output devices.

Inside the computer, a device called a processor receives the information and decides what to do next.

The processor works like a brain. It deals with all the information that goes into and out of the computer. It is small but very powerful.

HOW DOES AN ONLINE GAME WORK?

Online games send messages through the Internet. The Internet is a system that connects millions of computers around the world.

The Internet lets computers "talk" to each other. Information, such as words, pictures, and videos can be sent from one computer to another.

Online games use the Internet to connect players so they can share their moves.

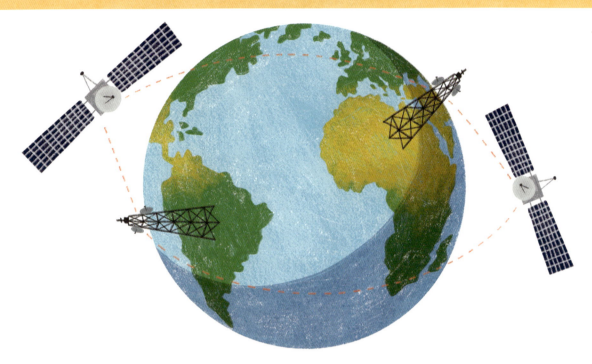

Computers can be connected in different ways. Some are linked by cables underground. Some use radio waves or connect to satellites—this is called a wireless connection.

Computers use the Internet to access websites. People can find information, do their shopping, and play games on websites.

WHAT MAKES A CAR MOVE?

Inside every car is an engine, which makes the car go.

Some cars use liquid fuel to power the engine. Burning the fuel moves parts called pistons up and down. Their movement is used to turn the wheels.

Some cars are powered by electricity, which is stored in a battery. Electric cars need to be plugged in to "charging points" to charge the battery.

As the pistons move up and down, they turn a part called the crankshaft.

The engine contains a row of pistons.

WHEEL

CRANKSHAFT

DRIVESHAFT

The crankshaft connects to a part called the driveshaft.

The driveshaft turns the wheels around, so that the car moves forward.

HOW DOES A MICROWAVE OVEN COOK FOOD?

If you want a quick, hot meal, put it in the microwave ... it will be ready in minutes!

Regular ovens cook by heating up the air around the food. In a microwave oven, food is cooked from the inside out.

Microwave ovens cook your food much quicker than ordinary ovens.

Inside a microwave oven is a magnetron. This sends out waves of energy called microwaves.

Microwaves make particles (very tiny parts) of water inside the food move quickly. This cooks the food.

A spinning fan bounces the microwaves around the inside of the oven and into the food.

MAGNETRON

HOW DOES A PIANO PLAY A TUNE?

A piano is a musical instrument with many strings inside. When you press a key, it makes the strings vibrate.

STRINGS

A guitar player plucks or strums the strings to create the sounds.

We hear sounds when an object vibrates, or makes small movements back and forth quickly. Musical instruments work by making vibrations in the air in different ways.

A piano can have around 230 strings. They are different lengths and thicknesses.

Short strings make high notes, and long strings make low notes.

When a piano key is pressed, a lever pushes a tiny hammer inside.

The hammer hits a string, which vibrates, making a sound. When the key is let go, a part called the damper moves down to stop the sound.

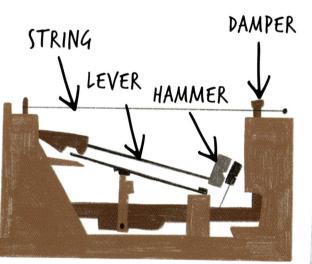

STRING

LEVER

HAMMER

DAMPER

KEY

WHAT MAKES A TOILET FLUSH?

When you pull the flush handle, parts inside a toilet work together to take away dirty water and replace it with clean water.

The toilet cistern, or tank, is filled with clean water.

Parts called valves let water into the cistern. They also stop the water when it is full.

When you flush, the cistern opens and water travels into the toilet bowl.

The clean water pushes the dirty waste water out through the waste pipe.

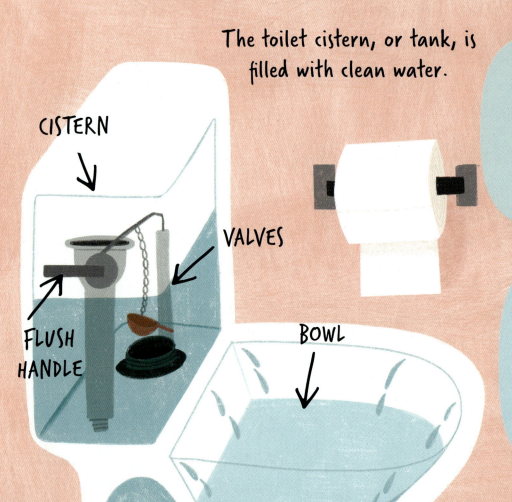

CISTERN

VALVES

FLUSH HANDLE

BOWL

WASTE PIPE

Clean water is pumped through large pipes underground. Water flows through smaller pipes into our homes.

Waste (dirty) water flows out through different pipes into drains. It goes to "sewage treatment plants" to be cleaned and used again.

HOW DO TRAINS STAY ON THE TRACKS?

Trains can be powered by steam, electricity, or diesel fuel. But all types of trains travel along tracks.

Most trains travel along two rails. The rails are made of steel, which is a very strong metal.

The wheels on each side of a train car are attached to a metal rod called an axle.

The axle keeps the wheels moving together and turning at the same speed.

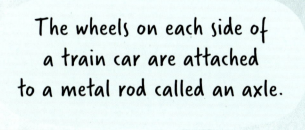

Each wheel has a rim called a flange. The flanges are slotted on the inside of the rail, which keeps them from moving outward and coming off the rail.

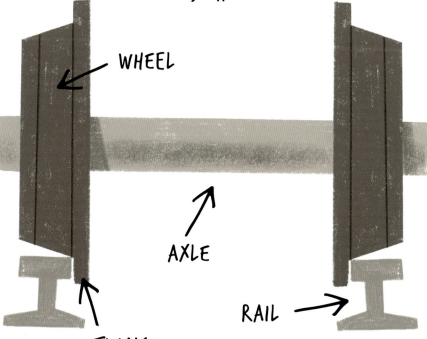

WHEEL

AXLE

RAIL

FLANGE

WHAT MAKES A HOT-AIR BALLOON GO UP?

Hot-air balloons are a beautiful sight, but how do they work?

Instead of an engine, a hot-air balloon uses something called a burner to make it fly.

CORD

BURNER

When the pilot turns on the burner, it heats up the air inside the balloon. Hot air is lighter than the cold air outside, so the balloon floats up.

To go down, the pilot pulls a cord that opens a flap at the top of the balloon. This lets out some hot air, which makes the balloon go down.

Balloons can be different shapes and sizes.

The rounded balloon part, called the "envelope," is made of tough fabric. It is filled with air.

There is a basket underneath that carries the pilot and passengers.

243

HOW DOES A HAIRDRYER DRY MY HAIR?

Hairdryers blow out hot air to dry your wet hair in minutes.

Hairdryers need electricity to work.

When a hairdryer is switched on, electricity flows to a small motor inside.

The motor makes a fan spin really fast.

FAN

NOZZLE

HEATING ELEMENTS

MOTOR

At the same time, parts called heating elements begin to warm up.

The fan sucks in cool air from the surrounding room and forces it past the heating elements.

The heating elements heat up the air, and hot air blows out through the nozzle.

HOW DO REFRIGERATORS KEEP FOOD FRESH?

Refrigerators work by warming and cooling something called a "refrigerant."

The refrigerant travels through pipes. The pipes run through the inside and outside of the refrigerator.

A part called the "expansion valve" changes the refrigerant from a liquid into a gas.

As it changes, the refrigerant takes away the heat from the inside of the refrigerator. This makes the refrigerator cooler.

As the gas leaves the inside part of the refrigerator, it flows through a type of pump called a "compressor."

PIPES

EXPANSION VALVE

COMPRESSOR

The compressor squeezes the refrigerant, turning it back into a liquid. The heat is released through the pipes at the back and into the air.

The refrigerant flows back up to the expansion valve, ready to start all over again.

WHAT MAKES A CLOCK TICK?

Clocks are machines that tell us what
time of day it is.

A traditional mechanical clock has a face, where the numbers are. The hands show the hours and minutes.

Inside mechanical clocks, weights and cogs work together to move the hands.

Mechanical clocks need to be wound up regularly. When we wind up a clock, energy is stored in a weight.

Special toothed wheels, called cogs, move the energy around the parts, causing the hands to turn.

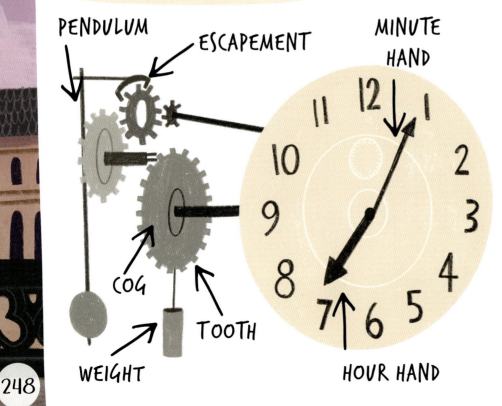

PENDULUM

ESCAPEMENT

MINUTE HAND

COG

TOOTH

WEIGHT

HOUR HAND

The escapement allows the cogs to turn, one tooth at a time. As each tooth moves through the escapement, it creates a ticking sound.

The pendulum is a swinging weight that controls how fast the teeth pass through the escapement.

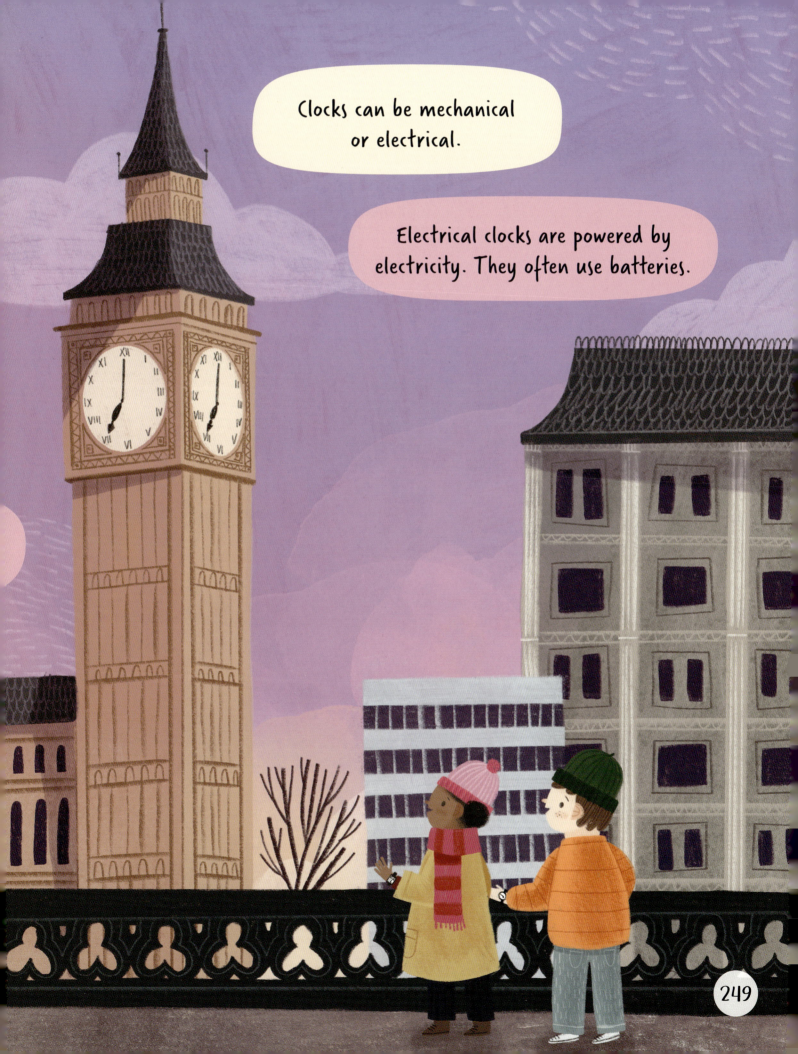

HOW THINGS WORK QUIZ

How well do you remember facts about how machines and other things work? Decide if these sentences are true or false, then check your answers on page 256.

1 Bicycle pedals are connected to a gear.

2 Some shoes stay fastened with hook-and-hoop fasteners.

3 Dishwashers need electricity and water to work.

4 Radio waves are invisible waves of energy that can travel through the air and space.

5 Helicopters can only fly forward and backward.

6 A computer processor acts like a brain.

7 Hairdryers need water to work.

8 Musical instruments work by making vibrations in the air in different ways.

GLOSSARY

Algae plantlike living things, usually found in water.

Antenna a pair of feelers on the heads of many creepy-crawlies.

Asteroid a small, rocky space object.

Atmosphere a shell of gases around a planet, star, or other object.

Avalanche a huge amount of snow, ice, or rocks falling quickly down a mountain.

Battery a means of storing electricity.

Bioluminescence an animal's ability to make light within its own body.

Blow hole the hole on top of a whale or dolphin's head, which is used for breathing.

Camouflage when an animal's fur or skin copies the patterns from nature to help them hide from predators.

Canopy the thick, leafy layer high up in the forest.

Comet a chunk of rock and ice from the edge of the solar system.

Coniferous to do with a type of tree with needles and cones.

Constellation a star pattern in the sky.

Continent one of earth's seven major areas of land.

Coral reef a large underwater structure made up of lots of hard coral joined together.

Coral tiny sea animals with a hard, outer skeleton. Together, their skeletons form reefs.

Crater a big hole in the ground.

Dam an obstacle across a river or stream to slow the water flow.

Deciduous to do with a type of tree that has leaves that drop off each year.

Dusk the time of day when it starts to get dark.

Electricity a type of energy. Machines that plug into sockets or have batteries use electricity.

Emergent layer the very top layer of the forest, where only the tallest trees poke up above the rest.

Energy the power to do things.

Environment the surroundings, including the living things and non-living things found there.

Evaporation changing from a liquid to a gas.

Explorer a person who travels in search of information about lands that are not well known.

Extinct (volcano) no longer active and will probably not erupt again.

Forest floor the lowest layer of a forest.

Fuel a substance, such as gasoline, petrol, or diesel, that is burned to make energy.

Fungi a group of living things that get their food from rotting material or other living things.

Galaxy a huge collection of stars, gases, and dust.

Gas a substance that is not a solid or a liquid. A gas spreads out and has no fixed shape.

Gear a wheel with "teeth" that connects to and turns another wheel.

Glacier a slow-moving mass of ice.

Hibernate to go into a deep, sleep-like state through winter to save energy.

Hunt to search for animals to eat.

Hurricane a very large, swirling, and windy storm.

Invertebrate a member of a group of animals without a skeleton in their bodies.

Lagoon a shallow lake or pool.

Mammal a member of a group of animals that has a backbone, has hair on its body, and feeds its young with milk.

Mate a partner for animals to have babies with.

Microphone a device that picks up sounds and turns them into electrical energy.

Microwave a wave of energy that can pass through food and heat it up.

Milky Way our home galaxy.

Moon a ball of rock that travels around Earth or another planet.

Motor a machine that is used to provide energy to move something.

Nest a place built by an animal for sleeping in and laying eggs.

Network a group of things that are connected, such as a computer network or a cellular phone network.

Orbit the path that an object in space takes around another space object.

Oxygen a natural gas in the air that all living things need to survive.

Planet a huge, round object that travels around a star.

Plankton tiny living things, including plants and animals, that float in fresh water or seawater.

Poison a substance that can kill or seriously harm living things.

Predator an animal that hunts and eats other animals.

Prey an animal that is hunted and eaten by other animals.

Radio wave an invisible wave of energy that can travel through the air and space.

Rain forest a thick, often tropical, forest where there is lots of rain.

Recycling taking used things, such as newspapers or bottles, and turning them into new things.

Reptile a member of a group of animals that usually have scales on their skin and lay eggs.

Rover a space robot that can move across the surface of a planet. It sends information about the planet to scientists.

Source the start of something, such as a river.

Star a giant ball of hot gas. Most stars look small in the sky because they are so far away.

Sun Our closest star, in the middle of the solar system.

Satellite any object that travels around a planet.

Seabed the bottom, or floor, of the ocean.

Shellfish invertebrate sea creatures that have hard outer shells, such as crabs and clams.

Silk a very thin thread made by some insects.

Solar system Our Sun, its eight planets, and their moons.

Tadpole a frog after it has hatched from an egg and before it grows legs.

Technology having to do with scientific inventions for practical use.

Tectonic plate a piece of Earth's crust that can rub against other pieces, causing volcanic eruptions and earthquakes.

Tentacles the long, thin parts of an animal usually used for holding and feeling. Some animals' tentacles can sting.

Tide the flowing of water away from or back onto the land.

Undergrowth the grassy, bushy layer of a forest.

Universe everything around us, including the world, space, and everything in it.

Valve an object that controls the flow of a gas or liquid.

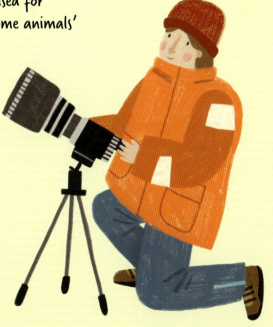

INDEX

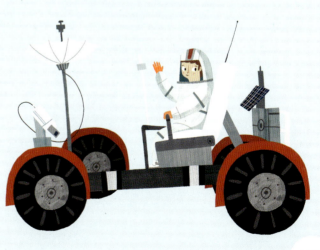

ANSWERS

Jungle Animals Answers

1 False—the female harpy eagle is almost twice the size of the male.   2 False—they have orange hair.
3 False—they move very slowly.
4 True.   5 True.   6 True.   7 True.   8 False—they have spots shaped like roses on their fur.

Woodland Animals Answers

1 False—they change from season to season.
2 False—they live in homes called lodges.   3 True.
4 True.   5 True.   6 True.   7 True.   8 False—they stay green all year round.

Our World Answers

1 True.   2 True.   3 False—it is very hot in Earth's inner core.   4 False—they cover more than half of the planet.   5 True.   6 False—a volcano that is extinct probably won't ever erupt again.   7 True.   8 False—they are formed over many millions of years.

Ocean Animals Answers

1 True.   2 False—sea otters live in groups.   3 False—tiger sharks are longer than a family car.   4 True.
5 False—they are highly poisonous to eat.   6 True.
7 False—sailfish are the fastest fish in the sea.   8 True.

Space Answers

1 True.   2 True.   3 True.   4 True.   5 False—it is a dwarf planet that is found beyond Neptune.   6 False—it appears blue.   7 False—it is the largest planet in our solar system.   8 True.

How Things Work Answers

1 True.   2 True.   3 True.   4 True.   5 False— helicopters can also fly backward and sideways.   6 True.   7 False— hairdryers need electricity to work.   8 True.